THE CONTROVERSIAL WORLD
OF BIBLICAL ARCHAEOLOGY
Tomb Raiders, Fakes, & Scholars

RELIGION & MODERN CULTURE
Title List

Born-Again Believers: Evangelicals and Charismatics

Color, Culture, and Creed: How Ethnic Background Influences Belief

The Controversial World of Biblical Archaeology:
Tomb Raiders, Fakes, and Scholars

The Grail, the Shroud, and Other Religious Relics:
Secrets and Ancient Mysteries

The Growth of North American Religious Beliefs: Spiritual Diversity

Issues of Church, State, and Religious Liberties:
Whose Freedom, Whose Faith?

Jesus, Fads, and the Media: The Passion and Popular Culture

Lost Gospels and Hidden Codes: New Concepts of Scripture

The Popularity of Meditation and Spiritual Practices:
Seeking Inner Peace

Prophecies and End-Time Speculations: The Shape of Things to Come

Touching the Supernatural World: Angels, Miracles, and Demons

When Religion and Politics Mix:
How Matters of Faith Influence Political Policies

Women and Religion:
Reinterpreting Scriptures to Find the Sacred Feminine

THE CONTROVERSIAL WORLD
OF BIBLICAL ARCHAEOLOGY
Tomb Raiders, Fakes, & Scholars

by Kenneth McIntosh, M.Div.

Mason Crest Publishers
Philadelphia

Mason Crest Publishers Inc.
370 Reed Road
Broomall, Pennsylvania 19008
(866) MCP-BOOK (toll free)

First printing
1 2 3 4 5 6 7 8 9 10

Library of Congress Cataloging-in-Publication Data

McIntosh, Kenneth, 1959–
  The controversial world of biblical archaeology : tomb raiders, fakes, and scholars / by Kenneth McIntosh.
       p. cm. — (Religion and modern culture)
  Includes index.
  ISBN 1-59084-983-3   ISBN 1-59084-970-1 (series)
  1. Bible—Antiquities. I. Title. II. Series.
  BS621.M42 2006
  220.9'3—dc22

                                2005010077

Produced by Harding House Publishing Service, Inc.
www.hardinghousepages.com
Interior design by Dianne Hodack.
Cover design by MK Bassett-Harvey.
Printed in India.

CONTENTS

Introduction   6

A Few Words to the Reader   8

1. Bible & Spade: What Is Biblical Archaeology
   & Why Does It Matter?   10

2. Ark-eology & the Search for Noah's Flood   22

3. The Father of All Believers: Abraham   34

4. The Search for Moses & the Exodus   42

5. Joshua & the Battle Over Jericho   54

6. The Age of Kings   64

7. The Dead Sea Discoveries & the World Jesus Knew   82

8. Fakes & Finds   100

Further Reading   108

For More Information   109

Index   110

Picture Credits   111

Biographies   112

INTRODUCTION

by Dr. Marcus J. Borg

You are about to begin an important and exciting experience: the study of modern religion. Knowing about religion—and religions—is vital for understanding our neighbors, whether they live down the street or across the globe.

Despite the modern trend toward religious doubt, most of the world's population continues to be religious. Of the approximately six billion people alive today, around two billion are Christians, one billion are Muslims, 800 million are Hindus, and 400 million are Buddhists. Smaller numbers are Sikhs, Shinto, Confucian, Taoist, Jewish, and indigenous religions.

Religion plays an especially important role in North America. The United States is the most religious country in the Western world: about 80 percent of Americans say that religion is "important" or "very important" to them. Around 95 percent say they believe in God. These figures are very different in Europe, where the percentages are much smaller. Canada is "in between": the figures are lower than for the United States, but significantly higher than in Europe. In Canada, 68 percent of citizens say religion is of "high importance," and 81 percent believe in God or a higher being.

The United States is largely Christian. Around 80 percent describe themselves as Christian. In Canada, professing Christians are 77 percent of the population. But religious diversity is growing. According to Harvard scholar Diana Eck's recent book *A New Religious America*, the United States has recently become the most religiously diverse country in the world. Canada is also a country of great religious variety.

Fifty years ago, religious diversity in the United States meant Protestants, Catholics, and Jews, but since the 1960s, immigration from Asia, the Middle East, and Africa has dramatically increased the number of people practicing other religions. There are now about six million Muslims, four million Buddhists, and a million Hindus in the United States. To compare these figures to two historically important Protestant denominations in the United States, about 3.5 million are Presbyterians and 2.5 million are Episcopalians. There are more Buddhists in the United States than either of these denominations, and as many Muslims as the two denominations combined. This means that knowing about other religions is not just knowing about people in other parts of the world—but about knowing people in our schools, workplaces, and neighborhoods.

Moreover, religious diversity does not simply exist between religions. It is found within Christianity itself:

• There are many different forms of Christian worship. They range from Quaker silence to contemporary worship with rock music to traditional liturgical worship among Catholics and Episcopalians to Pentecostal enthusiasm and speaking in tongues.

- Christians are divided about the importance of an afterlife. For some, the next life—a paradise beyond death—is their primary motive for being Christian. For other Christians, the afterlife does not matter nearly as much. Instead, a relationship with God that transforms our lives this side of death is the primary motive.
- Christians are divided about the Bible. Some are biblical literalists who believe that the Bible is to be interpreted literally and factually as the inerrant revelation of God, true in every respect and true for all time. Other Christians understand the Bible more symbolically as the witness of two ancient communities—biblical Israel and early Christianity—to their life with God.

Christians are also divided about the role of religion in public life. Some understand "separation of church and state" to mean "separation of religion and politics." Other Christians seek to bring Christian values into public life. Some (commonly called "the Christian Right") are concerned with public policy issues such as abortion, prayer in schools, marriage as only heterosexual, and pornography. Still other Christians name the central public policy issues as American imperialism, war, economic injustice, racism, health care, and so forth. For the first group, values are primarily concerned with individual behavior. For the second group, values are also concerned with group behavior and social systems. The study of religion in North America involves not only becoming aware of other religions but also becoming aware of differences within Christianity itself. Such study can help us to understand people with different convictions and practices.

And there is one more reason why such study is important and exciting: religions deal with the largest questions of life. These questions are intellectual, moral, and personal. Most centrally, they are:

- What is real? The religions of the world agree that "the real" is more than the space-time world of matter and energy.
- How then shall we live?
- How can we be "in touch" with "the real"? How can we connect with it and become more deeply centered in it?

This series will put you in touch with other ways of seeing reality and how to live.

A FEW WORDS TO THE READER

Some people believe biblical archaeology is more than history; they feel it can prove—or challenge—the Bible. Consequently, it can affect spiritual faith. If you have a strong belief in the Bible, you might feel uncomfortable reading statements by some of today's skeptical archaeologists. On the other hand, if you are skeptical of religion, you might find your views upset by the ways archaeology has supported the Bible. This book attempts to explain accurately what is happening today in biblical archaeology. Whatever you believe, there will be something in this book to confront or stimulate your thinking. That is what makes the topic so controversial—and so fascinating.

You may also wonder how this book fits into a series on spiritual trends in North America. What do ancient sites in Israel, Egypt, and Iraq have to do with America in the twenty-first century? For one thing, American scholars have always been in the forefront of biblical archaeology—and they still are. For another, discoveries made in the Middle East influence the beliefs of people throughout the world, and interest in these discoveries is especially keen in the United States and Canada. Finally, the United States has influenced biblical archaeology in a harmful—although unintentional way—due to looting and destruction of important sites during the war in Iraq.

In biblical archaeology, even words can become a source of heated debate. Arabs refer to the land between Egypt and Syria as Palestine. Jews call this land Israel. People die every day fighting over the land they call either Palestine or Israel. To honor the perspectives on both sides of this controversy, this book alternates between calling the land "Israel" and "Palestine," and sometimes the "Holy Land," a good term, since for both groups the land is indeed holy.

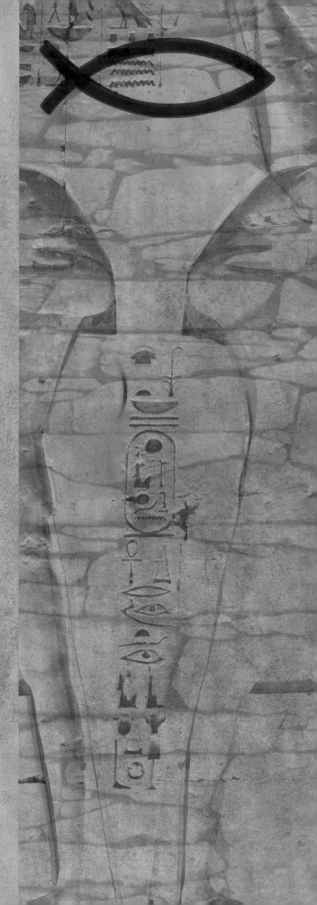

Chapter 1

BIBLE & SPADE
What Is Biblical Archaeology & Why Does It Matter?

"Take this—wave it at anything that slithers." Indiana Jones hands his beautiful associate Marion a torch.

"The whole place is slithering!" Marion snaps back.

They are in the Well of Souls, a hidden chamber in the ruins of an ancient Egyptian city, and hissing poisonous snakes surround them. Nazis have stolen Indiana's prize—the sacred Ark of the Covenant. The Germans have left Jones and his assistant in the well to die. The torches dim, and the deadly snakes crawl closer. Indiana and Marion have to find a way out—fast.

Indy spies a snake crawling out of a **petroglyph** on the side of the chamber. He steps toward it.

"Where are you going?" Marion shouts.

"Through that wall!" Indiana whirls his bullwhip around and lassoes the arm of an enormous statue. It is a frightening giant image of the jackal-headed Egyptian god Anubis. Indiana pulls himself up onto the head of the statue and rocks the towering idol back and forth until it comes smashing down through the wall—with Indiana on its back. Marion crawls through the hole toward daylight. They have beaten their way out of the deadly enclosure, and now they can resume pursuing the Ark.

ARCHAEOLOGISTS VS. TOMB RAIDERS

When many people think of biblical archaeology, they think of Indiana Jones. Harrison Ford portrays the scientist who is constantly fighting and charming his way through one peril after another in pursuit of ancient sacred treasures. Alternatively, you might think of Lara Croft, played by Angelina Jolie. Wearing form-fitting clothes and armed with rapid-fire weapons, she crashes and smashes her way through deadly traps to possess ancient *mystical* objects.

You might be surprised to learn that Indiana Jones and Lara Croft are not doing archaeology. They are tomb raiders or treasure hunters, adventurers who pursue prizes. They do not seem concerned about the destruction of ancient sites. Real-life tomb raiders are the curse of genuine archaeology. Treasure hunters destroy clues to the past in their pursuit of relics. Thousands of alleged biblical relics might be real or fake. No one can tell because tomb robbers did not record where and when they found them.

Archaeologists don't bust into a place. They work for months, or even years, examining and photographing a site inches at a time. Real-life archaeologists may not look as sexy as Harrison Ford or Angelina Jolie. Their lives aren't as action-packed as cinema heroes. Yet they seek something more valuable than gold or relics—priceless information about the past.

THE HISTORY OF BIBLICAL ARCHAEOLOGY

Scientific pursuit of the ancient Middle East begins with Sir Flinders Petrie. He discovered that *tels* (the Hebrew word for "heap" or "mound") are man-made hills covering ancient cities. Most important, he found a way to prove the dates of ancient Eastern archaeological sites. He found certain styles of broken pottery beside Egyptian relics of a kind he had previously dated. Thus, Petrie was able to define the ages of objects

14

"You call this archaeology?"

—Professor Henry Jones, after his son Indiana has finished a

shoot-out with Nazi soldiers, in the movie Indiana Jones and the

Last Crusade

buried in various layers of the ground. Petrie's stratigraphy—the science of establishing dates by layers—is the foundation of all Middle Eastern archaeology since his time.

In the 1920s, Sir Leonard Woolley and his companions captured the public imagination with amazing finds in Iraq. In the history of biblical archaeology, Woolley may come closest to the "Indiana Jones" image. He found treasures made of pure gold as he worked alongside Thomas Lawrence, a man who later became famous as Lawrence of Arabia. Lawrence was a competent archaeologist, but he was also spying on the German army for the British government. Agatha Christie, the famous mystery writer, stayed at their camp because she was dating Max Mallowan—another of Woolley's workers. They all lived in an enormous villa piled high with sheepskin rugs, ancient statues, and, as Mallowan described it, "gold scattered underneath our beds."

From the 1920s to the 1950s, biblical archaeology encouraged the faith of Bible believers. William F. Albright, for example, had amazing knowledge of both the Bible and archaeology, and he did not believe his discoveries did anything to contradict the Bible. Nelson Glueck, an archaeologist and rabbi who worked alongside Albright and surveyed more than 1,500 sites in the Holy Land, wrote, "No archaeological discovery has ever controverted a biblical reference." Those were the days when biblical archaeologists worked "with Bible and spade." They assumed their findings would match the Bible.

This approach changed with Dame Kathleen Kenyon, who excavated the Holy Land in the 1950s and 1960s. When she dug up the ancient city of Jericho, she declared that no city existed at the time when Joshua

lived. (If you're not familiar with the story of Joshua and the walls of Jericho, see chapter 5.) This was the first direct challenge by an archaeologist to the truthfulness of the Bible. It would not be the last.

AN IMPORTANT MODERN DEBATE

Today, several archaeologists claim the Bible is more myth than history. Israel Finkelstein, director of archaeology at Tel Aviv University, and Neil Silberman, who directs the Center for Archaeology in Belgium, have written a book titled *The Bible Unearthed.* They say the ***Exodus***, the conquest of ***Canaan***, and the glories of ***Solomon***'s empire are all fictional. Thomas Thompson, professor of Old Testament at Copenhagen, Denmark, published in 1999 *The Mythic Past—Biblical Archaeology and the Myth of Israel*, in which he claimed the entire Old Testament is fiction. Fellow scholars have dubbed Finkelstein, Silberman, and Thompson "***biblical minimalists.***"

The majority of biblical archaeologists disagree with the minimalists, considering their views too extreme. Ephraim Stern of Hebrew University says the minimalists "have nothing to do with reality." Lawrence Stager of Harvard University says the minimalists "haven't demonstrated a thing." Frank Moore Cross of Harvard University agrees: "I think the minimalist movement will . . . evaporate. You can't have something that's nonsense persist too long."

Those who say the Bible is almost all "myth" and those who claim it is "photographic history" are two opposite extreme views of biblical archaeology. Few scholars today stand in either of those two extremes. The debates rage over what to do with the vast disputed middle.

David Noel Freedman, famous for his writing in the field of biblical archaeology and for his scholarly work in Bible interpretation, believes the debate with the minimalists "will end somewhere in the middle."

SIR LEONARD WOOLLEY
A Man of Action and a Man of Patience

When a local official seized their passports and refused to return them, Leonard Woolley and Thomas Lawrence whipped out loaded revolvers. Woolley told the official, "In five minutes, one of two things shall be [on the table]—all of my papers, or your brains." The official handed back their documents.

Woolley could act decisively, yet he also displayed patience and painstaking precision, which made him a great archaeologist. When he found an ancient wooden harp, he knew as soon as he set eyes on it that he would destroy the object if he touched it—so he sealed it back in its hiding place until he could learn how to remove the precious instrument without damage. Four years later, he excavated the harp safely.

According to Freedman, "In my view, religion can tolerate historical in-accuracies in the Bible." Philip King, who has served as head of the Society of Biblical Literature and the Catholic Biblical Association, also holds a middle-ground view. He says archaeological methods cannot start with the Bible, "because you'll [just] find what you're looking for.

RELIGION & MODERN CULTURE

> *"In the past, there was a kind of prior commitment to the Bible: if the Bible says it, it's true. Now that is unscientific. On the other hand, to go to the other extreme—if the Bible says it, it's untrue—that's bad too. The truth lies somewhere in between."*
>
> *—Noted scholar David Noel Freedman, quoted in* Biblical Archaeology Review

. . . After you finish your work, then it's fine, you can look for correlations with the Bible."

Biblical archaeologists disagree on many things, yet they work toward a common goal: unearthing the past. The minimalists and those who disagree with them are a little like the two FBI investigators in the television show *The X-Files.* On the one hand, Fox Mulder was willing to believe in everything—UFOs, Bigfoot—you name it; the sign on his office said, "I want to believe." His partner, Dana Scully, was a doctor and a skeptic. Although one would believe anything and the other was constantly skeptical, they made a good team. Perhaps the world also needs both skeptics and believers to uncover the past buried beneath the sands of the Holy Land.

WHERE BIBLE AND SPADE MEET

The Bible and archaeology may influence one another in three ways:

1. Archaeology can *verify* the truth of Bible accounts. For example, 2 Kings 20:20 says, "Hezekiah . . . made the tunnel by which he brought water into the city." That was verified when the tunnel—with ancient Hebrew writing—was found in 1880.
2. Archaeology can *challenge* the truth of Bible accounts. For example, Dame Kathleen Kenyon claimed there was no city of Jericho at the time of Joshua.
3. Archaeology can *change* our understanding of the Bible. In numerous cases, archaeological discoveries have shed light on the scriptures. For example, in Genesis 16 Abram's wife Sarai has failed to bear children for him. She suggests he have sex with her slave so the servant will bear him a child. This sounds rather kinky to modern readers. However, archaeological finds show this was common, even expected. In the ancient city of Nuzi, diggers found a law tablet dating to the time of Abram. It says, "Should the wife prove to be childless she must provide her husband with a slave woman."

Chapter 2

RELIGION & MODERN CULTURE

ARK-EOLOGY & THE SEARCH FOR NOAH'S FLOOD

Amon sat idly in the tall grass, feeling the warm sun on his skin and watching his father's cattle graze. The big cow was going to have her calf soon, and Amon needed to keep a close eye on her at this vulnerable time. He looked across the wide field to his village, several dozen baked mud houses with thatched roofs. Beyond the village was the lake. Fishermen had dragged a dozen reed rafts up onto the shore.

On the beach beside them sat Noah's ship. It was enormous—way too big to maneuver around the lake and much larger than needed to fish or trade with the other villages. For years, the crazy old man had ranted and raved about how the world was going to change—how the lake would become an ocean and then cover the earth. Amon grinned, thinking how silly and unnecessary that big boat was.

Suddenly, the ground shook—and it kept shaking. A sound like thunder assaulted the young man's ears. Amon turned toward the sound. His blood froze in his veins.

A wall of water—three times the height of a grown man—was sweeping downward from the hills, like a vast blue carpet unrolling over the land. In a horrified instant, Amon realized that Noah wasn't mad after all.

Amon turned and ran as fast as he could toward the great boat. The thunder grew louder; the ground shook so hard the young man could barely stay on his feet. Then it hit him—a cascade of water that felt like a hundred stone hammers pounding on his back. The wave rolled Amon around and around. He gasped for air and flailed, unsure which way was up or down. A minute later, his head came above water. He could see debris, thatch from a roof, a bleating struggling lamb. The entire land had turned to ocean. Far away, he spied Noah's vessel bobbing on the waves with tiny figures atop the boat—Noah, his family, and their animals. Amon had the horrible feeling that they alone would live to tell the story of this catastrophic day.

For thousands of years, Noah's ark has fascinated Jews, Christians, and Muslims. The story of Noah and the ark is in the Hebrew Bible (the Old Testament) in the book of Genesis, chapters 6 through 9.

ARCHAEOLOGICAL DISCOVERIES RELATED TO THE FLOOD

Nowadays, as Nahum Sarna writes in his book *Understanding Genesis,* "The science of geology offers no evidence in support of the notion that the earth's surface was at any time . . . submerged . . . by flood waters." Nevertheless, 60 percent of U.S. citizens in a 2004 survey said they believe in Noah's ark and a global flood. Many **evangelical** Christians believe that a global flood happened.

GLOSSARY

conservative: In favor of preserving the status quo and traditional values and customs.

cuneiform: The earliest form of writing.

evangelical: A Christian belief that the Bible is the authority.

geological: Pertaining to the geology of a region.

localized: Confined to a restricted area.

Mesopotamia: The ancient land that is Iran and Iraq today.

Nineveh: The ancient capital of the Assyrian empire.

More than a century ago, archaeologists discovered the Bible flood story is not unique. In 1835, British diplomat Henry Rawlinson risked life and limb climbing cliffs in Iran in order to decipher ancient inscriptions. He succeeded in cracking the code of *cuneiform* writing, the written language of ancient *Mesopotamia*.

Rawlinson's discovery enabled his apprentice, George Smith, to make another discovery, one that created great public interest. In 1872, Smith pieced together an ancient baked clay tablet from *Nineveh*, dating from the seventh century BCE. The tablet contained a Babylonian tale called the Gilgamesh Epic. The Gilgamesh Epic includes the account of a flood, a great ship containing all living creatures, and a bird sent out at the end of the flood when the waters receded. It was

> *"Taking into consideration all the facts, there could be no doubt that the flood of which we had thus found . . . evidence was . . . the Flood on which is based the story of Noah."*
>
> —*Sir Leonard Woolley,* Ur of the Chaldees, *1929*

obviously similar to the Bible's account of the flood. To this day, opinions vary as to the relationship between the Gilgamesh Epic and the Bible. Some scholars believe the Babylonian story is the basis for the biblical account. Other scholars believe that both Gilgamesh and Genesis are independent retellings of an actual event.

Although most scientists no longer believe a global flood drowned the entire earth, archaeology has uncovered evidence indicating a large but *localized* biblical flood. In 1929, Sir Leonard Woolley and friends were digging in Iraq (see the previous chapter for more on their exploits), when Woolley found a layer of mud that seemed to have wiped out an ancient civilization. His wife Katherine exclaimed, "Well, of course, it's the Flood!" Woolley agreed.

A widespread local flood—rather than a worldwide flood—would not necessarily contradict the Bible. The author of Genesis may have been explaining the flood as it appeared to people at that time. Woolley wrote: "It was not a universal deluge, it was a vast flood . . . which drowned the whole of the habitable land between the mountains and the desert; *for the people who lived there that was indeed all the world.*"

Scientist-author Isaac Asimov provides an example of this sort of thinking when he points out the statement by ancient historians: "Alexander the Great conquered the world and then wept for other worlds to conquer." The long-ago historians meant that Alexander had conquered the entire world known to the Greeks of that time. Asimov notes, however, that in modern scientific terms, "Alexander conquered only 4 percent to 5 percent of the earth's surface."

DATING SYSTEMS AND THEIR MEANING

You might be accustomed to seeing dates expressed with the abbreviations BC or AD, as in the year 1000 BC or the year AD 1900. For centuries, this dating system has been the most common in the Western world. However, since BC and AD are based on Christianity (BC stands for Before Christ and AD stands for *anno Domini*, Latin for "in the year of our Lord"), many people now prefer to use abbreviations that people from all religions can be comfortable using. The abbreviations BCE (meaning Before Common Era) and CE (meaning Common Era) mark time in the same way (for example, 1000 BC is the same year as 1000 BCE, and AD 1900 is the same year as 1900 CE), but BCE and CE do not have the same religious overtones as BC and AD.

Hugh Ross, a **conservative** evangelical with a background in science, believes that when Genesis describes the flood as covering the earth, it does so "from Noah's perspective in Mesopotamia, not from a modern global perspective." He gives examples of similar wording elsewhere in the Bible: First Kings 10:24 says "the whole world sought audience with Solomon." Obviously, that only refers to the extent of the world known to the author. Tribes did not come from Australia or America to visit Solomon.

FLOOD GEOLOGY—IS MODERN SCIENCE ALL WET?

A small group of evangelical scholars at the Institute for Creation Research (ICR) claims that modern science is wrong about the flood. They believe there was indeed a universal deluge, which created the Grand Canyon and killed the dinosaurs. They refer to their version of science as "flood geology." Flood geologists attempt to reconcile science with their particular interpretation of the Bible. As evidence, they point to certain fossil finds and geological formations. They also point out that Native people as far apart as Australia and North America tell legends concerning a flood and a great ship. They believe these stories must express a common memory shared by ancient cultures around the globe. The majority of scientists doubt the ideas of the ICR.

RECENT DISCOVERIES—THE BLACK SEA FLOOD

Woolley was certain he had found the biblical flood, but later excavators found that Woolley's "flood" was not large at all. Archaeologist Elizabeth Stone wonders if Woolley might have exaggerated his discovery in order to continue receiving financial support from investors. Recently, however, new discoveries have provided a more impressive possibility for the biblical flood.

"The possibility that there was once a man who built a boat to save himself, his family and his livestock from a watery catastrophe has certainly gained a considerably greater credibility. . . . A massive flood event within the time that humankind has been building boats is no longer a matter of myth, but one of firm scientific and historical fact."

—Historian Ian Wilson, Before the Flood

In 1993, Columbia University scientists William Ryan and Walter Pitman began testing a new theory. **Geological** evidence indicated that around 5600 BCE melting ice caps caused global ocean levels to rise, and they believed the expanding Mediterranean Sea then burst through the Straits of Bosporus, creating the Black Sea. Using sound waves and core samples from drilling, Pitman and Ryan proved their theory. A vast flood flowing from the Mediterranean into a low area had indeed created the Black Sea 7,600 years ago.

This new discovery attracted the attention of undersea explorer Robert Ballard, famous for finding the *Titanic*. If this were the biblical flood, he reasoned, there would be evidence of ancient cultures beneath the Black Sea. Were people living there at the time? Ballard's undersea team went to work. They were not disappointed. Ballard's robot submarine located tools and pottery on the ocean floor—evidence of a world submerged by the flood.

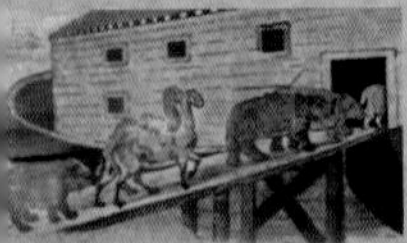

RELIGION & MODERN CULTURE

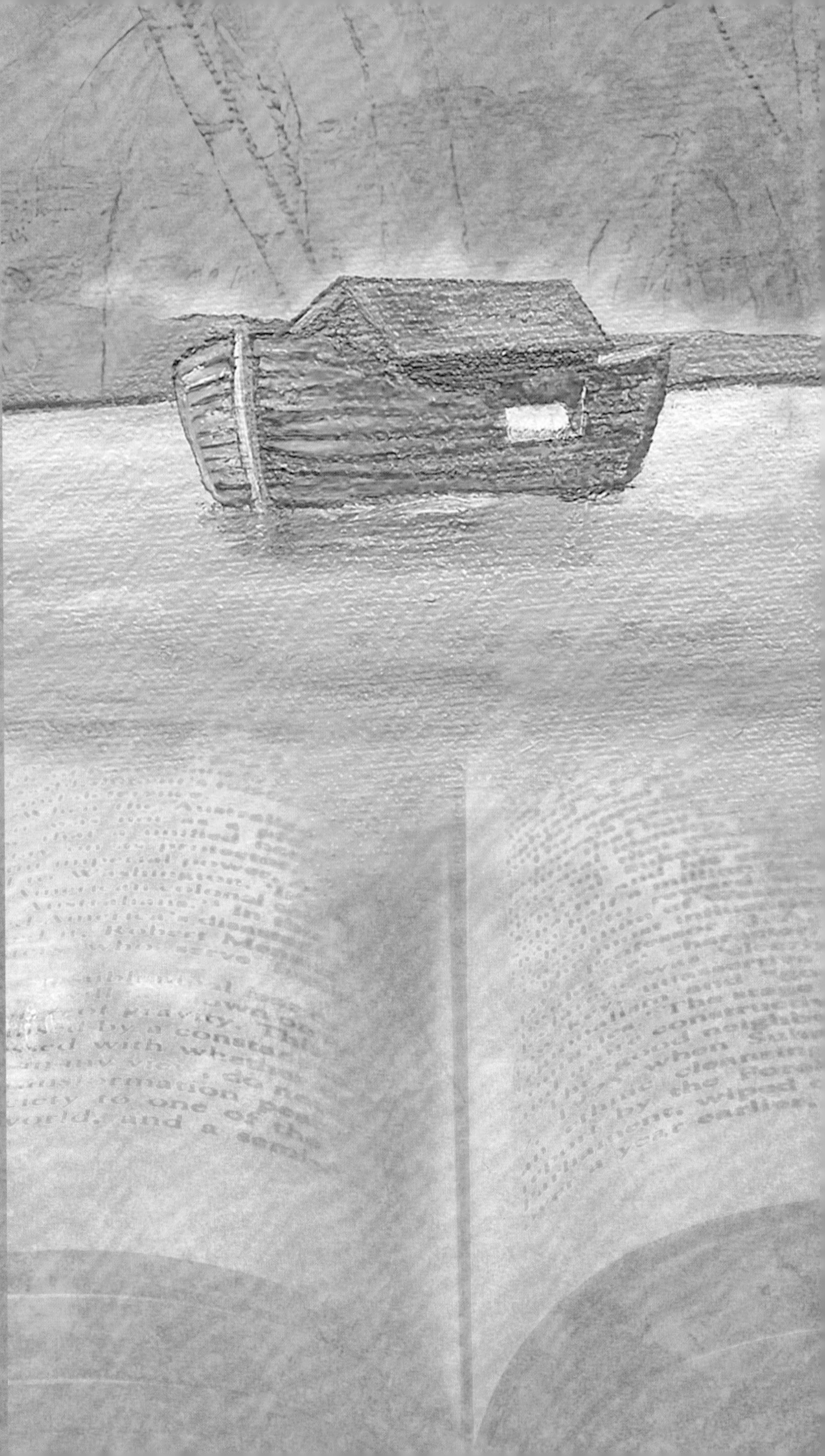

THE SEARCH FOR NOAH'S ARK, AN ARK-EOLOGICAL HOAX

In 1993, CBS made a documentary, *The Incredible Discovery of Noah's Ark*. On the show, a man named George Jammal displayed what he claimed to be an ancient piece of wood from Noah's ark, which he said he found on a mountain in Turkey. Jammal, an Israeli actor living in Long Beach, California, later confessed the wood was actually from some railroad tracks in Long Beach. He admitted he had never set foot in Turkey.

Ron Wyatt also attracted attention claiming to have found Noah's ark. Wyatt said the ark was now a stone formation approximately fifteen miles (24 kilometers) from the main peak of the Ararat Mountains. His "discovery" aired on the television programs *20/20*, the *Today Show*, and on the Discovery Channel. Skeptical investigators found Wyatt's claims to be utter fraud. Joe Zias, curator of the Israeli Antiquities Authority, says: "Mr. Ron Wyatt is neither an archaeologist nor has he ever carried out a legally licensed excavation . . . his claims . . . have no scientific basis whatsoever. . . . They fall into the category of trash which one finds in tabloids such as the *National Enquirer*. It's amazing that anyone would believe them."

What did happen to Noah's ark? While scientists may have uncovered proof of Noah's flood, it is unlikely they will ever dig up his ship. Wood is scarce in the Middle East, and residents of the ancient Near East usually dismantled large wooden objects so they could reuse the material. If there was an ark, it was probably recycled.

Chapter 3

THE FATHER OF ALL BELIEVERS
Abraham

The old man holds a jagged flint knife in trembling, gnarled hands. Before him, his teenage son lies on his back on a flat-topped boulder, trembling. They both believe in what others find impossible. God has spoken to this elder, repeatedly, and God has never failed him. Yet now, God has asked for the old man's dearest possession. "Go to Mount Moriah, and sacrifice your son, the one you love the most—Isaac."

"'Oh, he [Abraham] exists,' Professor Biran said. 'Just look around you. But remember, archaeology cannot prove or disprove the Bible . . . to me, these figures are real. I have no reason to doubt it. Whether all the details are correct, I don't know, and I don't really care. If you're looking for history you'll be disappointed. If you're looking for Abraham, you won't be."

—Avraham Biran, *a man regarded as the dean of biblical archaeologists, quoted by Bruce Feiler in* Abraham: A Journey to the Heart of Three Faiths

For years, Abraham and Sarah (also called Abram and Sarai) had prayed for a son. Isaac was their miracle child, born when Sarah was years past menopause. Now, God asks the unthinkable. Abraham knows the Canaanites in surrounding villages sometimes sacrifice their offspring to idols. He can only assume the Creator wishes to see how much Abraham trusts him—how far Abraham will go in obedience. Incredibly, Isaac is willing. That just makes Abraham love him even more—and dread even more what he must do.

Isaac allowed his father to bind him as he would a sacrificial goat. Now, the horrific moment has come. Abraham stands in slow motion, the knife sharpened and ready, steeling himself to slash. The son waits for his throat to be **sundered**. Abraham takes a breath, closes his eyes, draws back his arm, and then . . . he hears a voice.

"Stop! Do not do it. I see now that you truly fear me." Abraham

GLOSSARY

monotheistic: Belief in one god.

sundered: Broke apart or separated by violence.

drops beside the altar; the knife falls from his hand. Father and son both sob tears of relief.

The Hebrew Bible tells the story of Abraham in the book of Genesis chapters 12 through 25. The New Testament and the Koran also mention him. Two shrines in the Holy Land are dedicated to Abraham. At Hebron, the Haram el-Khalil (the Sanctuary of the Friend) sits atop the cave of Macpelah, where Abraham and family were buried (Genesis 25:9). The Dome of the Rock, in the very heart of Jerusalem's Old City, encloses the peak of Mount Moriah. There, according to Genesis 22, Abraham went to sacrifice his son. Although Jews, Muslims, and Christians revere these holy sites, the physical locations do not tell us much about Abraham or his world. For that, we must turn to archaeology.

IS SHE YOUR WIFE OR YOUR SISTER?
MAKE UP YOUR MIND

Ancient documents help us to understand Abraham's story better. Chapter 1 mentioned how the Nuzi tablets make sense of the "sex with slave" story. Likewise, it seems odd that three times in Genesis Abraham tells other men that his wife is his "sister." Recent translations of the Nuzi laws shed light on this problem. Ancient Mesopotamians had a custom called "wife-sistership." Sistership in this arrangement had nothing to do with blood relationships. A wife-sister had more legal privileges than a mere wife did. Genesis accurately records an ancient and long-forgotten custom from Abraham's time.

ABRAHAM & UR

Abraham's story begins in the city of Ur, in what is modern-day Iraq. The waters of the Euphrates River enabled civilization to develop in this area scholars call "the Fertile Crescent." Around 3000 BCE, the Sumerians developed the first form of written language when they used a wedge-shaped stick to mark on soft clay tablets. The inhabitants of

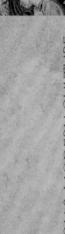

> *"Abraham is the shared ancestor of Judaism, Christianity and Islam. He is the linchpin of the Arab-Israelis conflict. . . . He is the father, in many cases the biological father—of 12 million Jews, 2 billion Christians, and 1 billion Muslims around the world. He is history's first monotheist. And he is largely unknown."*
>
> —*Bruce Feiler*, Abraham: A Journey to the Heart of Three Faiths

Mesopotamia used this style of writing—cuneiform—for the next three thousand years.

In the 1920s, Sir Leonard Woolley's crew unearthed gold-filled tombs and splendid palaces. They discovered that the ancient citizens of Ur enjoyed multistory apartments, paved streets, courthouses, and public libraries. Woolley wrote, "Abraham . . . was the citizen of a great city and inherited the traditions of an old and highly developed civilization." Sadly, the recent war in Iraq has destroyed a number of the treasures and archaeological sites found by Woolley.

The Bible stories of Abraham's life fit neatly with archaeological discoveries of customs in the Fertile Crescent around 2000 BCE. Finding evidence of Abraham the individual would be highly unlikely, like finding a needle in a haystack. What archaeology *has* found is evidence of his world, his customs, and his lifestyle. Though we may never find actual remains of this ancient desert wanderer, accounts of Abraham's life in the sacred scriptures continue to inspire believers in the three great **monotheistic** faiths.

Chapter 4

THE SEARCH FOR MOSES & THE EXODUS

"O divine majesty—there is a Hebrew shepherd from the desert who seeks audience with you. He claims to know you. Shall I dismiss him?"

Rameses the Great made no immediate reply. He was curious, but he did not like to display emotions. He was, after all, a god living among mere mortals. Slowly, he lifted one arm from his golden throne and made a slight beckoning motion. Two slaves leaped from their positions and ran to escort the visitor into the chamber.

Enormous cedar doors swung open on oiled hinges, and two dusty desert travelers strode into the chamber. They had weathered skin and carried shepherds' crooks. They were a sorry sight in the great hall covered with brightly colored **hiero-glyphs**, but they walked with dignity nonetheless.

op Maan... 's avonds
tuss en negh... nooit... ... Leeden
vo... preek...

... ... dag
in den Jaaren ... ... January ben ik
Joannes ... ... Juf ... in de Luthersche
Oude Kerck ... Domene ... Domene is getrou...

Geboorte en Naam Register onser Kinderen
in den Jaaren 1712 den 21 October 's morgens ten vier Uren
is mijn vrouw ... gekoomen me een dogter
dood Lijve

in den Jaaren 1715 ... November 's amiddags ...
twe en half ure ... is mijn vrouw in de kraan
gekoomen van ... Soon ... een huijs ...
Bernart Hendrik Emsighoff hoff gedoo...
van Hendrik getuijgen Syn Roeloff ...
vrouw Cristina Tillen den 3 ...

in den Jaaren 1714 den 23 april 's morgens tuss...
tien en tien Uren is mijn vrouw in...
van een dogter en is in de Oude Luth...
van domene Poulus wisselingh ... 29 ...
naam van Cristina getuijgen Syn Roe...
en huijs vrouw Cristina Tillen ... afm...

in den Jaaren 1716 den 28 December 's avons omtrent...
half ses Uren is mijn ... van een Soon in de kraa...
gekoomen ... Joannes everhardus Meijer...
in huijs ... van Jan Rudolf...
en syn ... Pieter en Maria...
ken ... ... vers, 29 dito gedoo...

The great king scrutinized the face of one shepherd. He seemed familiar. Those eyes—he had seen this man before, long ago. Then he remembered. Rameses spoke: "Moses? What brings you back to the place of your childhood? Last I heard, you killed a man and ran for your life into the desert."

Moses did not answer Pharaoh directly. Speaking with a husky but strong voice he demanded, "This is what Yahweh, the God of Israel, says: 'Let my people go!'"

DEBATES OVER THE ARCHAEOLOGICAL EVIDENCE FOR MOSES

The story of the Exodus has captivated readers for thousands of years. According to tradition, God gave Moses the Ten Commandments that provided a moral basis for *Western* civilization. Moviegoers throughout the world were thrilled when Charlton Heston spread his arms and a Technicolor ocean parted in the movie *The Ten Commandments*. More recently, the musical cartoon *Prince of Egypt* enthralled younger audiences. The original story of Moses is contained in the Torah (the first five books of the Hebrew Bible), in the book of Exodus.

Exodus is one of the best-loved stories of all time—but did it really happen? In *The Bible Unearthed*, Finkelstein and Silberman say, "Moses is just a myth." They point to the lack of archaeological evidence for Moses. Archaeologists have literally done tons of digging in Egypt, and they have never found any written documents regarding Moses or an escape of Israelite slaves.

Most biblical archaeologists do not believe this lack of evidence invalidates the Exodus accounts of Moses. Charles Pelligrino says, "That we do not read of Hebrews in Egyptian documents no more implies that they were not present than the fact that Egypt's pyramids are not mentioned in the Bible may be taken as proof that [the pyramids] never existed. *Absence of evidence is not always evidence of absence*" [italics added].

GLOSSARY

burning bush: A shrub that miraculously burst into flames and yet was not consumed by the fire; according to the story told in the Hebrew Bible, Moses heard God's voice speaking to him from the flames.

Egyptologist: Archaeologist who specializes in the study of ancient Egypt.

hieroglyphs: Ancient Egyptian writing using pictures or symbols.

scribes: People who copy or write out documents.

stele: A rock monument covered with writing.

Western: Found in, or typical of countries in Europe and North and South America, whose culture and society are influenced by Greek and Roman traditions and by Christianity.

The pharaohs controlled the way *scribes* recorded Egyptian history. The Egyptian rulers wiped out records of battles that were lost, embarrassing incidents, and political rivals. Omar Zuhdi, writing in *KMT: A Modern Journal of Ancient Egypt*, suggests Hatshepsut, one of Egypt's greatest rulers, may have been the pharaoh's daughter who rescued the baby Moses from the Nile. After Hatshepsut died, political enemies destroyed every record they could find that contained her name or her image. They tried to make history forget her. An escape of Hebrew slaves would be highly embarrassing to Egyptian royalty. If the Exodus really happened, Egyptians would not have recorded it.

"Take this staff, and do my wonders."

—God, *speaking to Moses in the movie* Prince of Egypt

Finkelstein and Silberman claim "the escape of [slaves] from Egyptian control at the time of Rameses II seems highly unlikely" because Rameses had immense military power. Yet that is exactly the point of the Bible story. According to Exodus, the escape from Egypt was more than "unlikely"—it was a divine miracle.

Finkelstein and Silberman believe, "The Exodus did not happen in the time and manner described in the Bible." Yet many other scholars say the Exodus story is credible. *Egyptologist* Ogden Goelet of New York University, writing in *Bible Review*, points out that Moses (or Mosis) is an Egyptian name. It would seem odd for the Bible writers to create an imaginary Jewish hero with an Egyptian name.

Exodus says Egyptian rulers forced the Hebrews "to build the cities of Pithom and Rameses as supply centers for the king" (Exodus 1:11). Kent Weeks, an Egyptologist at the American University of Cairo, is excavating the builders' quarters at Rameses. His excavations show that Rameses II did use foreign workers to build the city. Mansour Radwan, another Egyptologist, has examined workers' skeletons at other sites. The average laborer died at age thirty-five, suffering from arthritis and multiple fractures in his or her bones, evidence of hard, backbreaking physical labor.

The Merneptah *Stele*, a black stone with Egyptian writing on it, is an important piece of evidence for the Exodus. (Merneptah was the pharaoh after Rameses II.) This stele is the first document outside the Bible that mentions Israel, proving the existence of a nation called "Israel" somewhere in the direction of Canaan (modern-day Israel/Palestine) in 1210 BCE, just after the death of Rameses. The sudden appearance of Israel north of Egypt at that time fits perfectly with an escape from Egypt when Rameses was king.

The average laborer died at age thirty-five, suffering from arthritis and multiple fractures in his or her bones, evidence of hard, backbreaking physical labor.

FOLLOWING THE PATH OF THE ISRAELITE EXODUS FROM EGYPT

Researchers have attempted to trace the path of the Israelites fleeing Egypt. They did not cross the Red Sea as portrayed in so many Bible stories and movies. Long ago, Bible translators made a small mistake: the Hebrew words *Yam Suph* are not *Red Sea*, but rather *Reed Sea*. Where is the Sea of Reeds? In ancient times, the region north of the Suez to Lake Timsah was choked with reeds or marsh grasses. They called this body of water the Reed Sea.

In 2001, noted journalist Bruce Feiler followed the path of the Exodus. He believes Lake Timsah was the body of water through which the Israelites escaped from Egypt. He says: "For me, crossing Lake Timsah was an important goal. . . . A 16-year-old boy, Mohammed, agreed to ferry us across. 'I catch mostly gray mullet,' he said, 'or sometimes Moses fish.'

"'So what do you know about Moses?' I asked.

"'He was a prophet, wasn't he?' the boy said.

"'Yes. He split the sea. Do you think you can do that for us?'

"'Sorry,' Mohammed said. 'That's a miracle.'"

Feiler recalls, "For the first time since I started the trip, I felt myself start to cry."

IF YOU THINK YOU GET BAD WEATHER

Bible scholars have suggested nine of the ten plagues recorded in Exodus chapters 7 through 11 can be explained by a sequence of natural events. (The Bible plagues are in italics.)

1. Unusually heavy rains erode red dirt, which turns the *Nile red like blood* and kills the fish.
2. This causes *frogs* to move out of the river and swarm over the land.
3. Stagnant waters and decaying frogs cause multiplication of *gnats*.
4. *Flies* likewise multiply.
5. These insects carry anthrax from the rotting frogs, *killing the cattle*.
6. Humans also contract the deadly illness, causing *boils* on their skin.
7. *Hail and thunderstorms* are part of the unusual rain cycle.
8. Unusually heavy rains also cause hatching of *locusts*.
9. When the monsoons stop, soil erosion blows into sandstorms that can bring *darkness* over the entire land.
10. The final plague, however, is unexplained by science. The *death of the Egyptian firstborn* requires a supernatural cause.

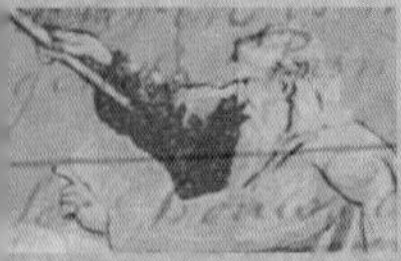

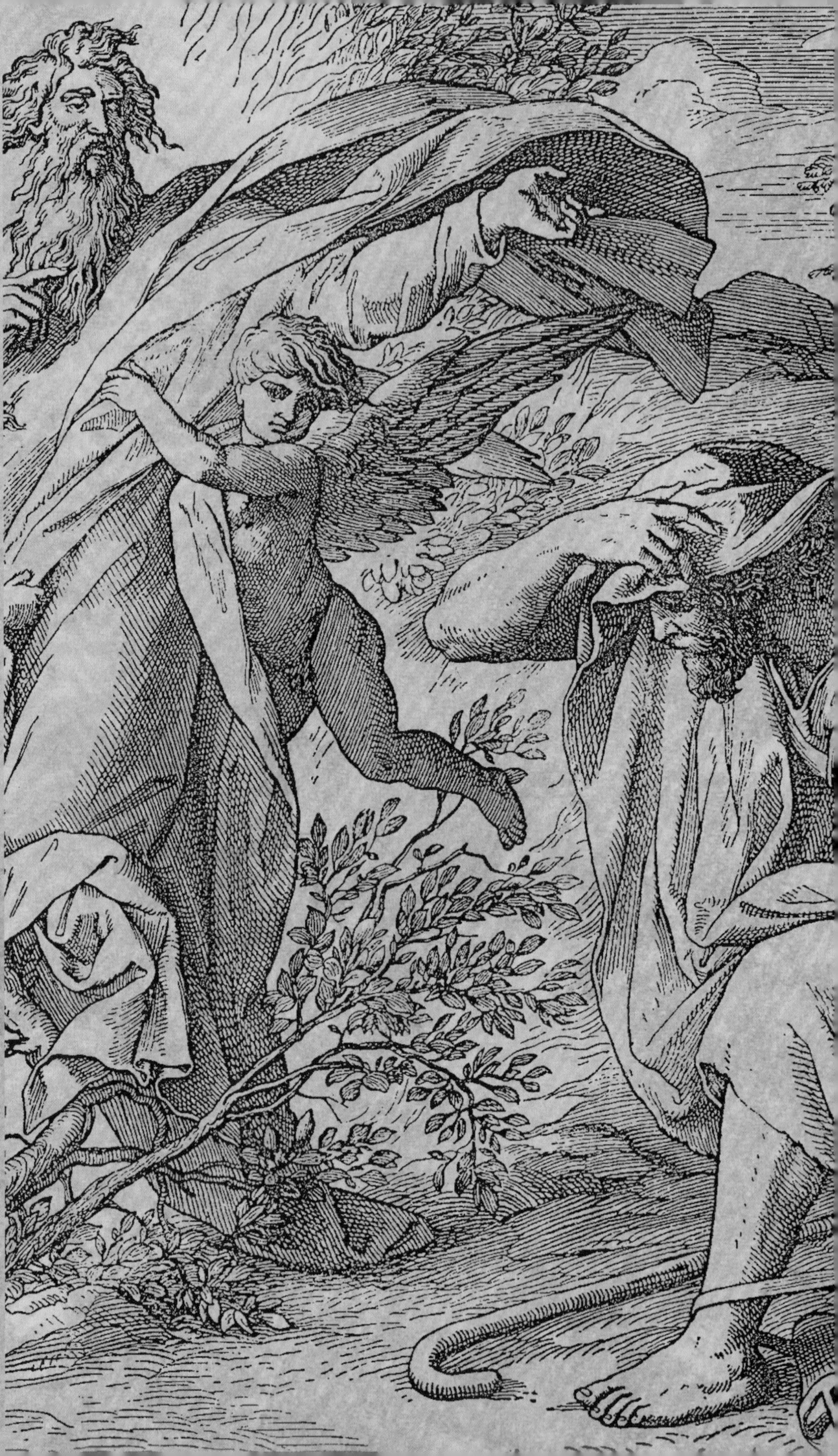

"Our society finds truth too strong a medicine to digest undiluted. In its purest form, truth is not a polite tap on the shoulder; it is a howling reproach. What Moses brought down from Mt. Sinai were not suggestions but ten commandments."

—Ted Koppel, journalist

SEARCHING FOR MOUNT SINAI

The book of Exodus says that after leaving Egypt, the Israelites journeyed to Mount Sinai, where God had spoken to Moses through the **burning bush**. There, God gave Moses the Ten Commandments. So where is Mount Sinai?

For 1,700 years, Christians have regarded a stark red granite peak in the south of the Sinai Desert as Mount Sinai. Local Arabs call the mountain *Jebel Musa*—the Mountain of Moses. Christian monks built a fortress-like monastery there in the fourth century. If you visit the monastery, the monks will show you an immense bush—the burning bush, they say. Though it may or may not date to the time of Moses, the monks have kept that same plant alive since 400 CE.

If you visit Jebel Musa, you must make an 8,000-foot (2,438-meter) climb from the monastery to the top of the peak. Gazing from the top of the mountain, you may feel strangely removed from the rest of the world. It is not just the thinning air; travelers who make the trek say the mountain is a uniquely spiritual place.

Nonetheless, scholars debate the location of Mount Sinai. An Italian archaeologist, Emanuel Anati, believes his excavations prove the mountain described as Mount Sinai in the Bible is in Israel, not Egypt. At Har Karkom, a bare mountain in Israel's Negev Desert, Anati found shrines and rock paintings. One petroglyph on Har Karkom portrays a staff transforming into a snake. Another piece of rock art shows two tablets

with ten distinct portions. Could this depict the Ten Commandments? Anati says his discoveries do not prove the Bible stories actually happened. Nonetheless, his finds at Har Karkom suggest a real basis for Moses and the Ten Commandments.

On the one extreme, some archaeologists say Moses is an unhistorical myth. On the other hand, others say the Bible accounts match archaeological clues. The debate will doubtlessly continue. In the meantime, memories of the Exodus provide hope for oppressed people everywhere. The Ten Commandments give moral direction to millions. Moses is more than a mere historical figure. His story continues to influence the world.

THE MOST FAMOUS MIRACLE OF ALL

Moses's parting of the Red Sea may be the most famous miracle in history. It has been the subject of countless paintings and several powerful movies. But what really happened?

Colin J. Humphreys, a renowned Cambridge University physicist with a long list of degrees and memberships in the most prestigious scientific organizations, published a book in 2003 titled *The Miracles of Exodus* in which he describes a rare natural event called "wind set-down." The Bible says a strong wind blew all night before the sea parted for Moses, and Humphreys demonstrates that a strong continuing wind can actually cause a large body of water to divide with a pathway down the middle—just as Exodus says the Red Sea opened for the Israelites.

Even if wind set-down can explain the crossing of the Red Sea, the deliverance of Israel still required a miracle. The waters parted just at the right moment for the tribes of Israel to escape, and the wind quit blowing at just the right moment to cut off the Egyptian pursuit. If this event actually occurred, it had to be a miracle of divine timing.

Chapter 5

JOSHUA & THE BATTLE OVER JERICHO

Sweat dripped off the faces of the men, women, and children who lined the ramparts and stood atop the roofs of Jericho. Not just the sweltering heat of this humid oasis caused them to perspire; their fear made them sweat. For seven days, the Hebrew tribes had surrounded the town. Jericho was under siege.

This was no ordinary siege, though. The Hebrews had done none of the things a city expected when attacked. Instead, for the past six days, the Hebrew army had walked around the city, blowing rams' horns, following a gilded box carried on poles. Was this some strange kind of trick?

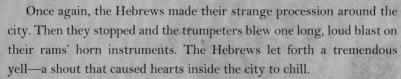

Once again, the Hebrews made their strange procession around the city. Then they stopped and the trumpeters blew one long, loud blast on their rams' horn instruments. The Hebrews let forth a tremendous yell—a shout that caused hearts inside the city to chill.

The ground began to vibrate. Shrieks of absolute panic filled the air. Children clutched at their parents' garments; faces became ashen with fear. The vibrations grew stronger, and then at almost the same horrific instant, the houses and walls came smashing down to the ground. Outside Jericho, the Hebrews let forth another shout, pulled out their swords, and ran straight over the fallen walls.

DID THE WALL FALL?

The Bible story of the fall of Jericho in the book of Joshua chapters 1 through 6 has been a favorite Bible story for many generations. Did it really happen?

Today the city of Jericho is a sleepy community located 825 feet (251 meters) below sea level. Arabs call it "the City of Palms." In the center of Jericho is the Tel, and under this enormous mound of dirt, archaeologists have found remains of the world's oldest civilization. Jericho's ancient remains spellbind archaeologists, but the public wants to know: is there evidence that the walls tumbled down?

Archaeologists Sellin and Watzinger excavated the Tel in 1907, and their findings disappointed Bible believers. They said there had been no city on the site at the time of Joshua.

In the 1930s, Professor John Garstang of Oxford was the next archaeologist to dig at Tel Jericho. Garstang believed he found evidence of the Israelites' conquest and of the collapse of the city described in the Bible.

Dame Kathleen Kenyon excavated Tel Jericho twenty years later. She worked more carefully than had archaeologists before her and discovered that at one time the city was tumbled by an earthquake. However, she said this happened centuries before the time of Joshua. Kenyon concluded there was no city of Jericho at the time of Joshua.

Not everyone agrees, however. In the past decade, archaeologist Bryant Wood has done further research at Jericho. He believes the dating of the Jericho site by Kenyon is incorrect. According to Wood, Joshua's army did fight the battle of Jericho.

So what can be concluded from all this disagreement? Archaeology reference books declare a draw in the battle over Jericho. Excavations neither prove nor disprove the story.

ISSUES CONCERNING THE ISRAELITE SETTLEMENT OF CANAAN

There is, however, a larger issue—Joshua's invasion of the Promised Land. Archaeologists generally agree this did not happen as it appears in the book of Joshua. That book seems to indicate that Israel rolled over Canaan in a quick series of devastating attacks. So when archaeologists began digging up Canaanite cities from the thirteenth century BCE, they expected to find numerous cities burned and *pillaged*. That was not the case.

*"Joshua fought the battle of Jericho, Jericho, Jericho,
Joshua fought the battle of Jericho,
and the walls came a tumbalin' down, down, down,
down."*

— *Gospel song*

Archaeologist William Devers, in *Eerdmans Dictionary of the Bible*, sums up the archaeological evidence (or lack of it) for Joshua's conquest: "Of the 16 Canaanite City states claimed to have been destroyed by Joshua's forces, a number have been identified and excavated, but only two—Bethel and Hazor—have produced any possible evidence for an 'Israelite destruction,' and even that is debatable."

Defenders of the book of Joshua point out that the conquest might not leave archaeological evidence. They also allege that mistakes have been made in the location or dating of sites.

Some archaeologists suggest there was a "gradual settlement" of Israel, rather than a sudden military conquest. This would fit with the account in the biblical book of Judges. Judges 1:19 reads, "The Lord was with the people of Judah, and they took possession of the hill country. But they failed to drive out the people living in the plains because they had iron chariots." This agrees with what archaeologists have discovered. Israelites lived in the hill regions from 1200 to 1000 BCE, but life continued without interruption in the Canaanite cities.

Adam Zertal of the University of Haifa has done more research on the settlement of the Promised Land than any other archaeologist. When Arab countries attacked Israel in 1973, a cannon shell hit Zertal, and he spent more than a year in a full body cast. Doctors said he would never walk again. Today, Zertal walks with crutches, but that does not slow him down. He has examined 220 archaeological sites.

Zertal believes his work proves the picture of Israelite settlement in the Promised Land as described in the book of Judges. Canaanites con-

"Archaeology without the Bible is archaeology without a soul."

—*Adam Zertal*

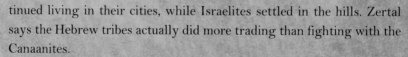

tinued living in their cities, while Israelites settled in the hills. Zertal says the Hebrew tribes actually did more trading than fighting with the Canaanites.

Other archaeologists question whether the Israelites actually moved into the Promised Land at all. They say the inhabitants of Canaan changed over time into what we now call Israelites. As proof, they point out that Canaanite and Israelite artifacts are very similar, if not identical. According to this view, the Bible books of Exodus and Joshua are myths created to provide a more exalted picture of Israel's past. But only a minority of archaeologists hold this viewpoint.

William Dever, professor of Near Eastern archaeology at the University of Arizona in Tucson, agrees that many of the Israelites were originally Canaanites. At the same time, he suggests there may have been a group that came out of Egypt. Dever believes the tribe of Joseph fled from Egypt led by Moses and settled among peasants in the hill country of Canaan. These Canaanites heard the stories of escape from Egypt and adopted the Exodus history as their own. Dever's view takes seriously both the Bible account of the Exodus and recent archaeological theories.

Archaeologists continue to disagree over Joshua, Jericho, and the invasion of Canaan. Every year or so someone writes a magazine article titled, "Archaeology Proves the Bible Is True," or—on the flip side—"Archaeology Proves the Bible Is a Myth." If the articles are talking about the early history of Israel, the reader should be cautious. Whatever you believe, don't get too excited. On these matters, the one thing we know for certain is this: The experts disagree with one another.

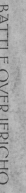

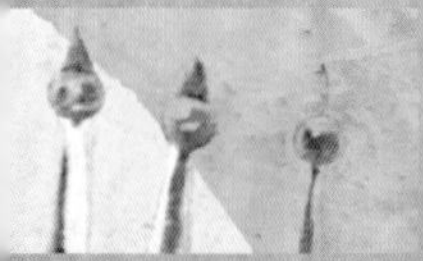

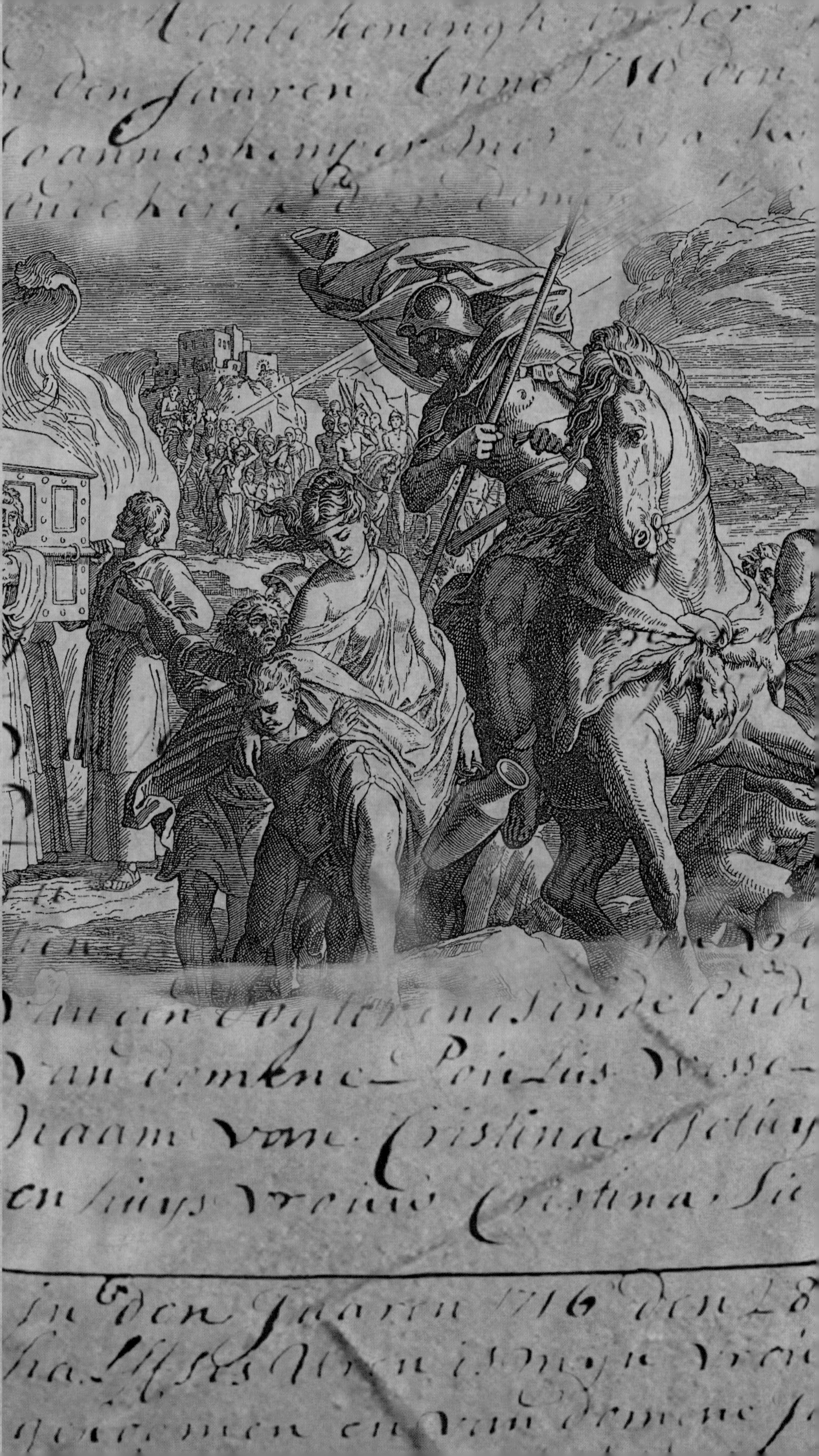

MODERN CONFLICTS & ANCIENT CONQUESTS COLLIDE

Archaeologists agree that the Canaanites, who lived in the Promised Land before the Israelites, had a highly advanced civilization. The Bible also portrays them as technologically superior to the Israelites. Who were these Canaanites? Do they have descendants still living today?

The people of the Holy Land in 2004 are bitterly divided. Arab Palestinians and Jewish Israelis struggle for control of a country each claim as their homeland. In the midst of this conflict, a few archaeologists have made an explosive sug-gestion. They say the Canaanites were the ancestors of today's Palestinians. Palestinians have welcomed this idea. It strengthens their claims to the land and suggests they came from an advanced ancient culture. At the same time, other archaeologists deny there is any proof for such a claim. In Israel/Palestine today, even theories about people who lived three thousand years ago can cause emotional and bitter conflict.

Chapter 6

THE AGE OF KINGS

RELIGION & MODERN CULTURE

She was the queen of a mighty empire, and she looked every inch the part. Layers of golden chains glittered against the dark skin of her neck, long fancy golden earrings dangled from her ears, and a golden crown sat heavily on her braided black curls. She wore layers of fine silk and cotton, dyed bright colors like the sun rising in the African dawn.

A procession of nobles and courtiers stood behind her, tall, muscular men who carried boxes full of gifts—priceless perfumes, exotic spices, finely carved elephant tusks, and precious jewels. Their queen's beauty outshone theirs.

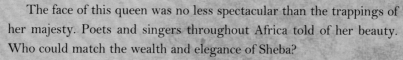

The face of this queen was no less spectacular than the trappings of her majesty. Poets and singers throughout Africa told of her beauty. Who could match the wealth and elegance of Sheba?

Yet, at this moment, she realized she had finally met a monarch who was her match—no, her superior. Solomon sat calmly above her on a throne carved entirely out of ivory and covered with gold. Guards and nobles stood in ranks, smiling at the procession from Africa as if they were everyday visitors.

As Sheba gazed at the king's face, she thought Solomon was the finest jewel she had seen. He, like she, seemed a perfect specimen of his sex. He was young and handsome, with a finely trimmed beard and curls of dark hair cascading down to his shoulders. His smile conveyed genuine warmth, and there was a twinkle in his eye. For the first time in many years, Sheba's heart skipped a beat.

She opened her mouth and said, "O King Solomon, I have heard many tales of your great wealth, your great kingdom, and your great person. All that I have heard does not do justice to your majesty, now that I behold it with my own eyes."

DID ISRAEL HAVE A GOLDEN AGE?

This scene sounds like it could come straight from a sexy romance novel. But did it really happen?

The Bible tells of a golden age in ancient Israel, the time when King David and King Solomon reigned. King David finished the conquest of the Promised Land and united the tribes into one empire. He built Jerusalem into a fine royal city. His son Solomon expanded the kingdom and built a great temple for God in Jerusalem—one of the wonders of the world. He raised a strong army, traded with nations throughout the earth, and acquired vast wealth.

For three thousand years the Jewish people have looked back on this golden age with a sense of pride. Israelites began as "the least of all people," poor, wandering shepherds. Yet they became, for a brief time, the mightiest ancient empire.

Now, however, a few archaeologists claim that it never happened. In his book *The Mythic Past*, Thomas L. Thompson writes, "Perhaps we might question whether Solomon really constructed his temple in Jerusalem. . . . Perhaps it was not Jerusalem but another city whose temple was important in history." Thompson claims David, Solomon, and the ancient kingdom of Israel are fiction. He points out that archaeologists have not unearthed any of Solomon's great buildings.

The majority of archaeologists are not surprised or troubled by this lack of evidence. They believe there are likely explanations for the lack

of physical evidence from the time of David and Solomon. The Bible says Solomon's Temple was destroyed by Babylon, rebuilt by Nehemiah, and then Herod built another temple over that one. Waves of conquest and expansion repeatedly destroyed and reconstructed the city of Jerusalem. Foreign kings took all the wealth of Solomon's empire. Considering what the Bible says about Jerusalem's later history, it would be surprising if anything from the time of David and Solomon survived. Archaeologists say evidence for the royal period of Israel's history exists elsewhere.

Digs in the cities of Meggido and Gezer have unearthed ruins dating to the time of David and Solomon. Eric Cline, associate professor of ancient history and anthropology at George Washington University, is excavating Megiddo, and Bill Broadway writes about the Meggido dig in an article for the *Washington Post*; he quotes Cline's professional opinion of the biblical minimalists' claims that the empires of David and Solomon are only myth: "These guys are nuts."

One piece of evidence refutes Thompson's claim that David existed only in fiction. In August 1993, news of an important archaeological discovery appeared in the international press after archaeologists found an ***Aramaic*** inscription from the ninth century BCE at the site of Tel Dan, in the extreme north of Israel. The tablet mentions Israel and the "house of David." This inscription confirms David's existence and suggests his influence extended far beyond Jerusalem.

ANCIENT CLAIMS & MODERN DISPUTES— THE TEMPLE MOUNT

It would be easier to agree about what happened in the ancient past if people living in Jerusalem today did not argue so bitterly. Jews, Muslims, and Christians have deeply divided claims and opinions,

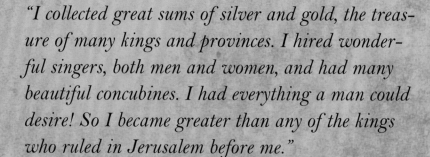

"I collected great sums of silver and gold, the treasure of many kings and provinces. I hired wonderful singers, both men and women, and had many beautiful concubines. I had everything a man could desire! So I became greater than any of the kings who ruled in Jerusalem before me."
—Ecclesiastes 2:8–9, New Living Translation Bible

especially about a sacred area in the heart of Old City Jerusalem. On top of that sacred area is the Dome of the Rock, a Muslim mosque, and on the side of the area is the Western Wall. Male Jews from around the world gather at all hours to pray aloud there, and all Jews may leave written prayers in cracks in the wall. Jews and Arabs alike consider this space to be the center of the world, and they are not happy to share it with each other.

Jews believe the Dome of the Rock is built over Solomon's temple. In the middle is a large rock surface archaeologists believe was the Holy of Holies. In the Hebrew Bible, God said his presence would dwell forever in this place.

For Islam, this is the Noble Sanctuary, from which Mohammad journeyed to heaven. A great golden dome and ornate mosque sit atop Mount Moriah. The entire area is holy ground for Islam, so visitors must cover up any revealing outfits and remove their shoes.

Some *fundamentalist* Christians believe someone must remove the mosque and build another Jewish temple over it in order for Jesus to return. Israeli authorities have accused Christian *fanatics* of plotting to destroy the mosque.

The Dome of the Rock may be the most bitterly contested piece of real estate on Planet Earth. There are certain limited hours when non-Muslims may enter the mosque. When those hours are over, a speaker

A ROYAL SCANDAL—AND HISTORY'S GREATEST STOLEN TREASURE CASE?

The Bible says the Queen of Sheba visited King Solomon, exchanged compliments, and then returned to her home. Ancient traditions, however, add more spice to the story. They say the Ethiopian queen and Jewish king were sexual partners. The Falashas, Jews who have lived in Ethiopia since ancient times, claim to be the offspring of Solomon and Sheba.

There is an even more intriguing twist to that story. According to ancient Ethiopian tradition, Sheba asked Solomon to give her a special gift, a copy of the Ark of the Covenant. Solomon was happy to do so, but the Queen of Sheba had a trick up her sleeve. Just before she left Jerusalem, the queen arranged for her servants to switch the duplicate Ark with the real thing, which they did secretly. The Ethiopian delegation left the phony Ark in Jerusalem, and unknown to the Jews, they took the genuine Ark of the Covenant home with them to Ethiopia. They say it remains there today.

calls out, "Jews—Christians—leave! Leave! It is our time now." Visitors leave the spiritual environment inside the mosque, with its thick Persian carpets and breathtaking architecture. They put on their shoes and walk out the gates. Israeli soldiers and Palestinian police officers, all carrying automatic weapons, stand on opposite sides of the exit. The Dome of the Rock/Temple area is a treasure they must defend relentlessly.

If you understand how controversial this site is today, you will understand why its ancient history becomes controversial as well. Recently, Palestinians have denied that this is the site of Solomon's Temple. "It's self-evident that the First Temple is a fiction," says one Palestinian archaeologist at Bir Zeit University. "The Second [Temple] also remains in the realm of fantasy." If David and Solomon are myths, if the Jews did not have a Jerusalem Temple in ancient times, then Palestinians would have a stronger claim to the city today. Most scholars say denial of the ancient Jewish Temple is entirely unjustified. This debate will not, however, be settled by digging, *carbon dating*, or publishing papers. In Jerusalem's old city, the past will only be resolved after people learn to live harmoniously in the present day.

JERUSALEM UNDER SIEGE—721 BCE

The inhabitants of Jerusalem felt both fear and hope. Outside their city a great army was encamped. The Assyrian army of King Sennacherib surrounded them. The Assyrians had moved through the east like devouring locusts, destroying city after city, slaughtering their residents. The messengers of Sennacherib shouted dire warnings to the inhabitants of Jerusalem: "What god of any nation has saved them from Assyria? Name just one! So what makes you think the Lord can rescue Jerusalem?"

"King Solomon became richer and wiser than any king in all the earth. . . . The king made silver as plentiful in Jerusalem as stones."

—*2 Chronicles 9, New Living Translation Bible*

The king of Jerusalem, Hezekiah, was a man of great faith. As the Assyrians prepared siege engines and planned their attack, he put on sackcloth and lay praying in God's temple. The prophet Isaiah encouraged the king and the people. Isaiah promised, "The Lord will protect this city from the king of Assyria. His armies shall not enter Jerusalem. The Lord is passionate about his people, and He will defend them."

Then, a miracle occurred. One morning, cries of grief came from the Assyrian camp. The soldiers hastily packed their belongings and quickly moved away from the city. On the ground, they left thousands of rotting bodies. A terrible disease had struck the Assyrian camp. The Lord had rescued Israel.

This account comes from 2 Kings 18 and 19. It's a dramatic story—but did it really happen? Archaeology suggests it did. At the Oriental Institute Museum in Chicago, a baked clay object is on display. It has six sides covered with cuneiform writing—and it is a description of a military campaign made by King Sennacherib in 689 BCE. Repeatedly, Sennacherib lists a city and then says, "I besieged, I captured, and I took away their spoils." Regarding Jerusalem, Sennacherib wrote, "Hezekiah King of Judah . . . I shut up like a caged bird within Jerusalem." He does not say he besieged or conquered the city. Oriental rulers did not like to record their failures. The fact he did not conquer the city fits perfectly with the biblical account of rescue by disease.

Archeologists found a record made by the king of Assyria reading, "I besieged and conquered Samaria [capital of the northern kingdom] and led away as booty 27,290 inhabitants."

ARCHAEOLOGICAL FINDS AFFIRM THE BIBLE HISTORY OF KINGS AFTER SOLOMON

After David and Solomon, the Bible tells how the tribes of Israel split into two separate kingdoms—Israel in the north and Judah in the south. For this era, there is an abundance of archaeological evidence. These finds verify numerous historical accounts in the Bible.

The Bible says Jeroboam, the king of Israel, "placed calf idols . . . in Bethel and in Dan. This became a great sin, for the people worshiped them, traveling as far even as to Dan" (1 Kings 12:29). Archaeologists have done extensive digging at Tel Dan, in the north of Israel. Today, it is an archaeological park. Visitors can stroll for hours looking at the tree-shaded remains of the ancient metropolis while Israeli F-14 fighter planes occasionally roar overhead, patrolling the boundary of nearby Syria. At the highest point of the ancient city is a temple and altar that archaeologists have identified as the site of Jeroboam's idols.

From 738 to 722 BCE, Assyria fought a devastating series of wars against Israel. The "Black Obelisk" from Nimrud commemorates the victory of an Assyrian king over Israel's King Jehu. The obelisk pictures the Jewish king kissing the ground in front of the Assyrian king. It is the only picture of an Old Testament king dating from ancient times.

Assyria destroyed the northern Kingdom of Israel in 721 BCE. Archaeologists found a record made by the king of Assyria reading, "I besieged and conquered Samaria [capital of the northern kingdom] and led away as booty 27,290 inhabitants." The Bible records the same sad event in 2 Kings chapter 18.

AN ARMY CHAPLAIN WORKS TO RESCUE THE ANCIENT CITY OF BABYLON

Captain Emilio Marrero is an American Baptist chaplain with the U.S. Armed Forces in Iraq. He cares for the spiritual needs of U.S. soldiers and Iraqi citizens. He is also the official caretaker for the ancient city of Babylon.

When he first saw the ancient site, looters were pillaging it. Concerned, Marrero went to his commanding general and asked for soldiers and a fence to protect the site. The army placed security around ancient Babylon. Marrero realized, however, that this created more problems: "An immediate side effect of enclosing the compound was the reality that the local populace had no means of generating income. . . . We needed to respond to their needs to build trust and instill hope for the future of their country."

Chaplain Marrero then began working with local villagers to establish a *souk* (a sales bazaar) so they could make money. Four months later, over fifty Iraqis had opened small businesses there. Marrero protected an important archaeological site and helped poor Iraqis earn an income. Most important, according to Chaplain Marrero, by doing these things he helped Iraqis and Americans trust each other more.

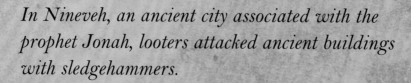

In Nineveh, an ancient city associated with the prophet Jonah, looters attacked ancient buildings with sledgehammers.

TRAGEDY IN IRAQ

Babylon's king Nebuchadnezzar took the captured residents of Jerusalem to Babylon, in what is modern-day Iraq. The book of Daniel describes this. Archaeologists working in Iraq have found all sorts of splendid things made during Nebuchadnezzar's reign. The nation of Iraq contains some of the most important archaeological sites in the world. During the twentieth century, archaeologists excavated approximately 10,000 sites in Iraq, unearthing tons of important artifacts. The archaeological significance of Iraq underscores the tragedy of recent events there.

When America and her allies entered Baghdad, observers accused U.S. troops of standing by while looters stole priceless artifacts from the Baghdad Museum. According to an August 2004 *Newsweek* article, "More than 8,000 pieces are still missing, of which almost 30 are considered of unique historical and artistic importance."

Meanwhile, treasure hunters pillage archaeological sites in Iraq every day. In Nineveh, an ancient city associated with the prophet Jonah, looters attacked ancient buildings with sledgehammers. The breakdown of law in the country, combined with a lack of jobs, has led to continuous looting. As one looter explained to a *Newsweek* reporter, "We are poor people." Looters make $10 to $15 selling artifacts to intermediaries who export them overseas. The same artifacts sell for thousands of dollars in Europe, the United States, and Asia. Once looters steal objects from an archaeological site, its use as a research tool is compromised, and it can never again yield information about the past that it could convey if it were untouched.

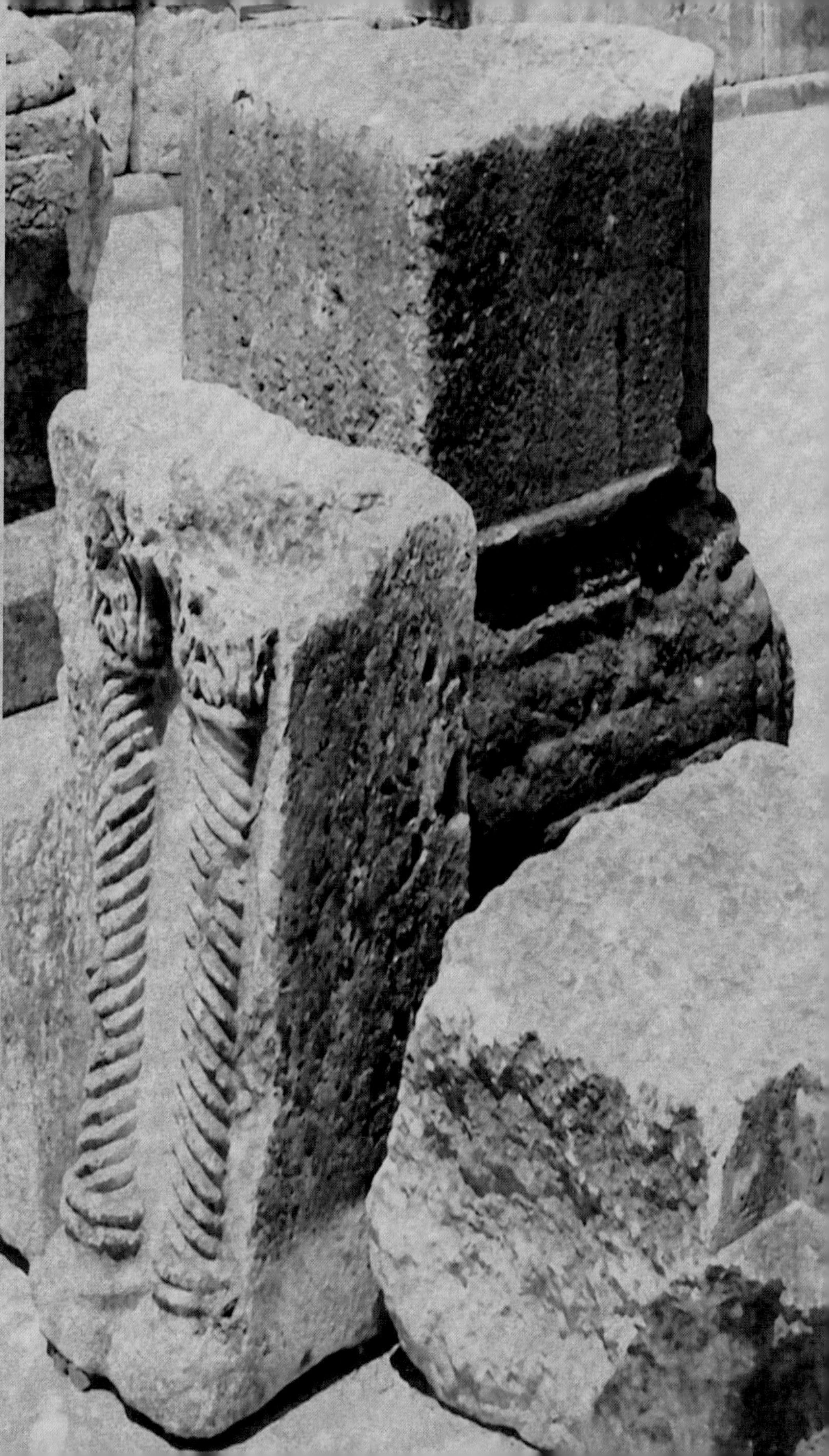

In a land where suicide bombings and beheadings are common, it is hardly surprising that the treasures of the past are vanishing quickly.

The interim Iraqi government has made efforts to save archaeological sites. However, one official explains why such efforts are largely futile: "Four men pull up in a pick-up truck, and they are armed: What are you going to do? Is the guard going to lay down his life for antiquities?" In a land where suicide bombings and beheadings are common, it is hardly surprising that the treasures of the past are vanishing quickly.

As Melinda Liu and Christopher Dickey say at the conclusion of their *Newsweek* article, "For archaeologists, for the faithful, for all of us, the loss of this past impoverishes the future. Ripping artifacts from their contexts takes away the last chance we have to know these civilizations—from the world of Abraham to that of Nebuchadnezzar—that gave us our own."

Chapter 7

THE DEAD SEA DISCOVERIES & THE WORLD JESUS KNEW

In 1947, three **Bedouin** shepherds were following their goats near the Dead Sea, in the desert southeast of Jerusalem. When a few goats headed up a steep hill, one shepherd, Juma Muhammed, followed. He noticed two small openings in the side of the hills—caves—and wondered if there might be treasure hidden in them. He threw a rock in the hole.

Crash! It was the sound of broken pottery. Now he was excited. He could just imagine ancient clay vessels filled with gold and silver. It was getting dark, however, and the cave would have to wait.

ם עَנפים דקים בَשעה 8 וחצי כדי לשזור זרים. הע

וגם מהענפים וגם מהَענَפים לَא שזרו זר. אך אנו

ד. בשעה 8 וחצד. בשעה 8 וחצי התכנסנו למסיבת

ם שחזרו. נَעים ֡ם שחזרו. נَעים היה לראות אותם ח

ים. ביד אחת הם. ביד אחت הרימו את הבן ובשني

החיילים שחזן החיילים שחזרו סיפרו במסיבה ו

אה שאפילו ד. אה שאפילו ד. התבגר. הבטתי על

Two days later, another shepherd, Muhammed Ahmed el-Hamed, woke early in the morning and decided to explore the caves. He found pottery jars with covers on them. Trembling with excitement, he opened one of the jars. He reached inside and pulled out an old rolled-up parchment. He opened the other jars with the same results. Crestfallen, he took some of the scrolls to show his companions. It was a letdown. The cave contained no silver, no gold, only old pieces of rolled-up leather and *papyrus*.

One of the shepherds took the scrolls to Bethlehem, hoping to sell them. A cobbler named Kando paid five pounds for the scrolls. Kando, a Syrian Orthodox Christian, took the scrolls to his archbishop, Athanasius Samuel, who became excited as soon as he saw the scrolls. He showed them to several experts—who declared them fakes. Eventually, however, photographs of the scrolls reached the famous American archaeologist William F. Albright. Albright realized they were ancient and unique.

By this point, however, Archbishop Samuel had become a laughing-stock. He wanted to get rid of the scrolls and raise some money for a charity. Therefore, in June of 1952, he placed an advertisement in the *Wall Street Journal*: "Biblical manuscripts dating back to 200 BC are for sale." A Mr. Sidney Esteridge from New York bought all of them for $250,000. Fortunately, Mr. Esteridge was a front for the Israeli government. Today, the scrolls are on display in a beautiful museum, called the Shrine of the Book, in Jerusalem. They are part of the collection of manuscripts known as the Dead Sea Scrolls.

THE DEAD SEA SCROLLS

The Dead Sea Scrolls are a collection of documents written in Hebrew, Aramaic, and Greek, composed between 250 BCE and 68 CE. They provide unique information about the Bible and Jewish history.

GLOSSARY

Bedouin: A nomadic Arab in the desert regions of Arabia and north Africa.

Essenes: A Jewish religious sect of the first century CE.

papyrus: Writing material made from the stem of the papyrus plant.

pilgrims: Those who travel to a holy place for religious reasons.

The scrolls come from caves in the area around the Dead Sea. Fed by springs and streams, this salty lake is the lowest point of the world. The waters of the Dead Sea are ten times saltier than that of the Mediterranean Sea. Nothing can live in the Dead Sea, and objects placed in the water will not sink, all because of the extreme salt content. Swimming in the Dead Sea is not much fun, though. When you get out of the water, it feels like your whole body is covered with oil.

The desert around the Dead Sea is a foreboding place, but a community once lived there. This was the Qumran monastery. They chose this harsh environment as a place to flee from the sinful world and devote themselves to God. Qumran community members were all men, and they avoided contact with women. They followed strict rules—and if someone broke the rules, other members would cast him out to face the desert wilderness.

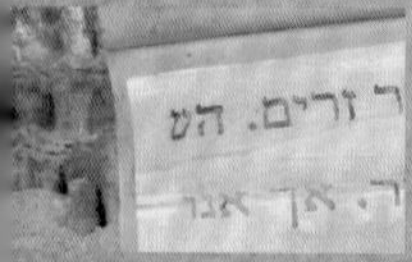

ר זרים. הע
ר, אן אנ

...כדי לשזור זרים. הע

...נפים לא שזרו זר. אך אנו

...רחצי התכנסנו למסיבת

...ים היה לראות אותם ח

...זרים את הבן ובשנין

...רו סיפרו במסיבה וו

...התבגר. הבטתי על

The Qumran community was part of a larger Jewish group called the **Essenes**. The Essenes avoided the Jerusalem Temple, believing that the Temple priests had departed from following God. The Essenes believed the end of the world would come soon. If they lived pure and holy lives, God would deliver them in the Final Judgment. Many scholars believe John the Baptist was an Essene who left the Qumran community.

The Qumran community wrote down many things on scrolls, which they stored in the caves. Today, the Dead Sea Scrolls consist of eight hundred documents. Most of these documents, however, came in piles of tiny, damaged pieces. Imagine eight hundred different jigsaw puzzles, all of which are missing some pieces and none with a picture to show you what they are. That will give you an idea of what a huge task it has been to put together the Dead Sea Scrolls. Furthermore, scholars have to translate them from ancient languages.

THE STRUGGLE TO MAKE THE SCROLLS PUBLIC

Cave 4 at Qumran yielded approximately fifteen thousand pieces of scrolls, about 40 percent of the entire Dead Sea Scroll collection. A team of eight young scholars began the task of putting the scrolls together and interpreting them, but there were no Jews among them. They were all Catholic except one, and he quit soon after the project began. This

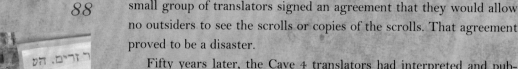

small group of translators signed an agreement that they would allow no outsiders to see the scrolls or copies of the scrolls. That agreement proved to be a disaster.

Fifty years later, the Cave 4 translators had interpreted and published only a tiny fraction of the manuscripts. These now-aging scholars clung greedily to their scroll fragments, allowing no one else to see them. Many other Bible scholars were disgusted at this hoarding of information. In 1985, the magazine *Biblical Archaeology Review* began a six-year campaign to free the Cave 4 scrolls. The issue was suddenly and surprisingly resolved in 1991. Few people knew that the Huntington Library in California owned photographs of all the Cave 4 fragments. Fed up with the secrecy of the translation team, the Huntington Library released copies of the scrolls to the world. The Dead Sea Scrolls from Cave 4 were no longer secret.

WHAT THE TRANSLATED SCROLLS HAVE REVEALED

So what have the Dead Sea Scrolls revealed? They give valuable insight into the Jewish world before 70 CE. Some outlandish ideas have circulated in the media—references to Jesus Christ and aliens from outer space—but actually, the scrolls contain nothing shocking or sensational.

The scrolls do show us that early Christians shared beliefs in common with Jews in the first century. The Qumran community practiced baptisms and ritual meals, similar to the early Christian church. There are Dead Sea Scroll sayings comparable to Jesus's Sermon on the Mount. At the same time, the Dead Sea Scrolls also clarify how Christians were uniquely different from Jews in the first century. No other group claimed that an actual person—a peasant from Galilee, no less—was the Son of God.

ח לֹא שזרו זר אַךְ

וְהִתכנסו למסיבּה

ם היה לראות אותם ח

הרימו את הבן ובמשני

ר סיפרו במסיבה וו

הבטחי על

There are Dead Sea Scroll sayings comparable to Jesus's Sermon on the Mount. At the same time, the Dead Sea Scrolls also clarify how Christians were uniquely different from Jews in the first century.

The most important contribution of the Dead Sea Scrolls has been in regards to the accuracy of the Hebrew Bible. Before the Dead Sea Scrolls, the oldest copy of the Hebrew Bible dated from the ninth century CE. That is at least 1,400 years after the scriptures originated. Critics suggested there must be drastic changes to the Bible over that long span of time—but the Dead Sea Scrolls proved there was little difference in the Hebrew Bible between 200 BCE and 800 CE. Words were changed here and there, and a paragraph was missing from one book, but they were mostly the same. This finding proved Jewish scribes had copied from manuscript to manuscript carefully, faithfully passing the words of scripture from generation to generation.

YESHUA AND HIS DISCIPLES ENTER JERUSALEM—30 CE

There is excitement in the air as crowds surge up the hill toward the temple. They line up at the *mikvahs*—ritual baths—to purify themselves before entering the holy sanctuary. They walk past the tomb of the Prophetess Huldah and begin their ascent of the "Teaching Steps," stairs that lead to the Triple Gate. This is the one sacred way for pilgrims on feast days—such as this Pesach (Passover) celebration—to enter the temple.

A REAL-LIFE TREASURE MAP

Real-life archaeology is not like an Indiana Jones movie; there are rarely clues to a hidden treasure. Yet, one Dead Sea Scroll is just that. Scholars call it the Copper Scroll, and it is the only Dead Sea Scroll made out of metal. The Copper Scroll gives detailed instructions on where sixty-five different hordes of treasure are hidden. Added together, the treasures are more than a hundred tons of silver and gold. Archaeologists believe this was the treasure of the temple in Jerusalem. Priests hid it when the Romans attacked.

Of course, researchers have followed the instructions on the Copper Scroll hoping to find that treasure. None of the sixty-five locations has yielded any treasure. What is wrong? There are two different problems involved. First, there are Greek letters placed within the Hebrew instructions—probably a code. So far, no one has cracked that code. In addition, the very last of sixty-five directions mentions another scroll containing additional information. Researchers believe the other scroll gives clues needed to understand the Copper Scroll. Thus far, the second scroll remains hidden. Therefore, the Copper Scroll, on display now at the Amman Museum in Jordan, remains a tantalizing unsolved mystery.

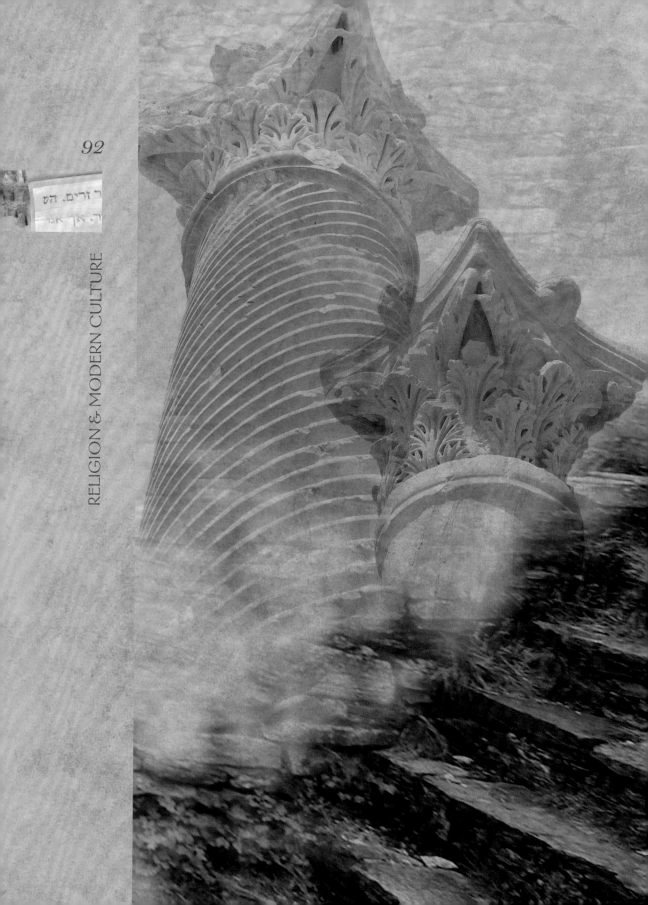

RELIGION & MODERN CULTURE

As they enter the gates, pilgrims gaze upward at the gold-covered ceiling of the inner temple. Even those who have made this pilgrimage before catch their breath. What nation on earth has a temple as glorious as this?

A Galilean rabbi and his students are in the center of the crowd walking into the temple. This peasant, Yeshua, has gained considerable notoriety. There are wild rumors. Some say he has done miracle cures. There are darker rumors, as well. He claims to be a king, and the Romans see him as a threat. Even in their holy temple, the Jewish people cannot escape from the strong arm of Rome. At the far end of the temple sits the Fortress Antonia, where armed legions stand ready to sweep down into this temple if they believe Imperial power is being provoked.

One of Yeshua's disciples pulls at the sleeve of his master's tunic. "Look, Rabbi, what marvelous stonework—what splendid marble columns and gilded tiles!" The disciple is a poor fisherman from the north, and he has never seen such sights. Yeshua stops and turns to face his followers. His little band pauses halfway up the steps, feeling nervous.

Yeshua speaks with frightening intensity. "You see these great buildings? I tell you, the time will come when Israel's enemies shall destroy everything you see today! Oh, Jerusalem—if only you would listen to my message of peace. But no, this great temple shall be shattered—and the Son of Man shall be put to death in this city."

Yeshua turns and walks resolutely up the steps into the temple. His disciples follow, wondering and fearing what will happen to them this week. Their teacher's words have filled them with foreboding.

The four Gospels of the Christian Bible—Matthew, Mark, Luke, and John—contain the stories of Jesus (Yeshua) and his followers.

Almost two thousand years after the time when Jesus of Nazareth lived, a group of Bible students and scholars enter the Ophel Archaeological Gardens. This site lies to the south of the Dome of the Rock, the site of the ancient Temple. Their guide, an archaeologist working in Israel, leads the group onto the Teaching Steps, the stairs that led up to the temple. They pause in front of three archways, now completely filled in with bricks. He tells them this is the Triple Gate, where Jesus and his disciples had to enter the Temple during the feast of Passover. He says, "You are standing in one of the few places where we believe Jesus would have walked."

Archaeologists have uncovered a number of the places where the Bible says Jesus lived and taught. The Gospels describe the village of Capernaum, on the shores of the Sea of Galilee, as home base for Jesus and the disciples. Israelis call the town Kfar Nahum (the Village of Nahum). Excavations at Kfar Nahum have uncovered a first-century home, later converted into a church. It is possible that Jesus and his followers might have lived in that house, and Christians might have built a church there later to preserve the memory of Jesus's presence. Archaeologists have also uncovered a first-century synagogue at Kfer Nahum. The Gospel of Mark chapter 1 says Jesus taught in that synagogue.

Archaeology can establish the credibility of Bible stories but it cannot prove them. Ancient records establish the existence of a man named Jesus. Archaeology proves the world described in the New Testament existed. It cannot prove that miracles happened, or that Jesus uttered certain words on certain occasions. No one was there with a camcorder to film Bible events.

For thousands of Christian *pilgrims*, the most important site related

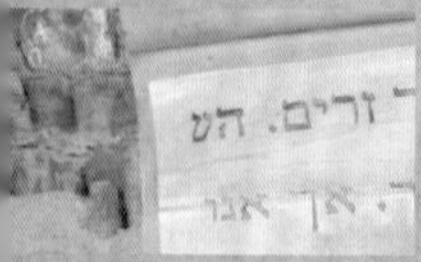

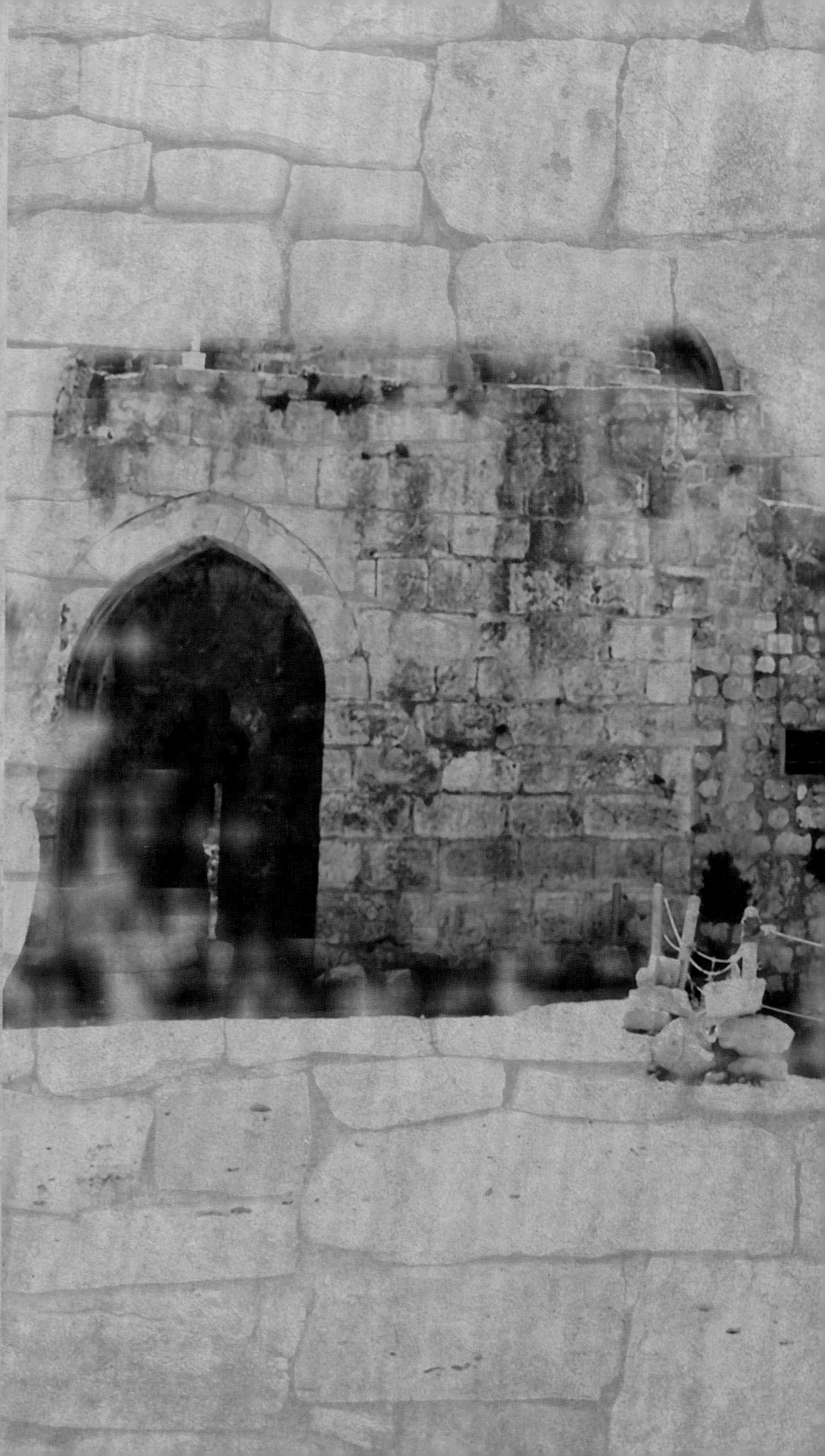

THE CAVE OF JOHN THE BAPTIST?

In August of 2004, archaeologist Shimon Gibson made a momentous claim. He says a cave near Kibbutz Tzuba contains a pool in which John the Baptist performed baptisms. He suggests Jesus himself may have received baptism there. Other archaeologists are skeptical. Hershel Shanks, editor of *Biblical Archaeology Review*, says "the evidence is thin" that John the Baptist used this site. For one thing, the Bible says John baptized in the Jordan River, but says nothing about a cave.

to Jesus is the Church of the Holy Sepulcher in Jerusalem. The church is actually a series of ancient, enormous buildings connected to one another. In the fourth century, the Empress Helena traveled from Rome to Jerusalem, and according to tradition, God gave Helena dreams revealing the place of Jesus's crucifixion and burial. She ordered the Church of the Holy Sepulcher built over those two spots. Pilgrims to the Holy Land believe that a hole in a stone surface marks the place where soldiers erected the cross of Jesus. Nearby, an ornate marble chapel surrounds the empty tomb where believers say Jesus was buried and rose again.

ר זרים. הע
ר. אך אבו

The ancient Jewish writer Josephus refers to Jesus in his history book, *Antiquities*, written in the first century after Christ's life:

> At this time there was a wise man called Jesus, and his conduct was good, and he was known to be virtuous. Many people among the Jews and the other nations became his disciples. Pilate condemned him to be crucified, and to die. But those who had become his disciples did not abandon his discipleship. They reported that he had appeared to them three days after his crucifixion, and that he was alive. Accordingly, he was perhaps the Messiah, concerning whom the prophets have reported wonders. And the tribe of the Christians, so named after him, has not disappeared to this day.

Does the Church of the Holy Sepulcher mark the real place of Jesus's death and burial? Archaeologists say it is possible. There is archaeological evidence that Jews used the site for burials in the first century. At the same time, there is no way to prove this particular site was that of Jesus's burial.

Like most articles of faith, the holy nature of the Church of the Holy Sepulcher is a matter of belief, not something science can prove. Archeology cannot give definite proof about the spiritual world. But it can offer exciting clues that help believers and nonbelievers alike have a better understanding of the world that shaped both Judaism and Christianity.

Chapter 8

FAKES & FINDS

The November 2002 edition of *Biblical Archaeology Review* hit the newsstands with one of the most exciting headlines in the history of the magazine: "World Exclusive: Evidence of Jesus Written in Stone." The article explained: "Amazing as it may sound, a limestone bone box (called an 'ossuary') has surfaced in Israel that may once have contained the bones of James, the brother of Jesus." It went on to explain that this ossuary had an inscription on the side, written in ancient Aramaic script: "James, son of Joseph, brother of Jesus."

Though biblical archaeology has done much to establish information about the world of the Bible, it has produced little evidence of Bible characters. For some Christians, the James Ossuary was the next best thing to the **Holy Grail**. It seemed that here was real evidence of Jesus.

Far ...
not to be sp...
Unseemly is praise on a sinner...
for it is not accord... to him in...
But praise is offered by the wise man's tongue;
its rightful steward will proclaim it.

Man's Free Will

... "It was God's doing that I fell away";
... what he hates he does not do.
... "It was he who set me astray";
... is no need of wicked m...
... ...dm... the LORD hates...
... ...it by all those who f...
... the beginning, created...
...made him... to his own ch...
choose you can... ...p th... command...
loyalty to do his will...
are set before you... ...waters...
whichever you... ...ch... forth...
... ...and death.
... chooses shall...
... wisdom of the...
... in power, and a...
... ...d see all he has...
... ...nds man's every d...
... does he command to...
... ...one does he give strength...

Punishment of Sinners

... for a brood of worthless child...
... ...e in wicked offspring,
... ...hey be, exult not in...
... not the fear of the...
... their length of life,
... in their future...
... be better than a thousand...
...childless than have godless ch...
...wise man can a city be pe...
...son of reb... a t...
...ming... has my eye se...

a Jn 4, 10.
b Sir 6, 26
c Jas 1, 13
d Gn 1, 27
e Dt 30,
f Pss 33,
13.

B. hold, the...
he... ...
his...
The rocks of the...
earth's...
at his mer...
Of no... ...ber...
...way... wa...
... no eye can...
... ...ll in secret...
...who tells him of...
and what could I...
Such are the thoughts...
which only the foolish...

1, 21: Sinful offspring
...perience show how G...
...ording to his deeds...
...man at his hand...
For Korah and...
...pointed Israelites...
The leaders...
... ...the flood...
The people of...
the Canaan...
The Israelites...

"In an age of digital scanning, even a teenager with average computer skills and the right software can resize and reproduce an ancient script more precisely than an expert scholar ever could do by hand."

— *Neil Asher Silberman and Yuval Goren*, Archaeology

Hershel Shanks, editor of *Biblical Archaeology Review*, revealed news of the find to the world at a press conference just before his magazine article came out. Trained as a lawyer, Shanks had examined the evidence for the ossuary before releasing the story. He consulted two experts in ancient biblical epigraphy, the science of studying writing. The two experts agreed the style of writing dated to the first century CE and was typical of that used in the Holy Land at that time. Shanks also had the ossuary examined by geology experts. They confirmed that the ossuary was made of limestone from the Holy Land, and materials on the surface of the ossuary dated to the first century. In light of the evidence, Shanks wrote, "We have here the first *epigraphic* mention—from about 63 CE—of Jesus of Nazareth." The ossuary was displayed at a museum in Quebec, Canada. Many people from Canada and the United States came to see an object they believed provided a tangible connection to Jesus.

DOUBTS EMERGE ABOUT THE OSSUARY

The James Ossuary seemed too good to be true. According to the majority of archaeologists today, it *was* too good to be true. From day one, there were concerns about the finding of the ossuary. The owner was a

GLOSSARY

epigraphic: Pertaining to the study of ancient inscriptions.

Holy Grail: The cup used by Jesus at the Last Supper and by Joseph of Arimathea to collect his blood and sweat at the crucifixion.

private collector in Israel named Oded Golan, who had bought the ossuary from excavators at an unofficial dig. He had no way to prove where and when it had been found. In archaeology, an artifact loses most of its value after being taken out of the ground—unless finders carefully document the excavation. Since there was no record of the finding of the ossuary, some archaeologists were dubious.

Just months after the James Ossuary came to light, another amazing relic emerged. This was the "Jehoash Inscription," a piece of gray stone slab with fifteen lines of Hebrew-Phoenician script that experts dated to 900 BCE. The text was very similar to a passage from the book of Kings in the Hebrew Bible. Again, Bible believers were ecstatic. Here was more proof of the Bible's historicity.

Archaeologists, however, quickly noted problems with the Jehoash Inscription. Famous epigrapher Joseph Naveh of Hebrew University said the alphabet on the inscription mixed symbols from the ninth century BCE with symbols used centuries later. Frank Cross of Harvard found errors in spelling and grammar and declared the stone was a forgery.

BIBLIA
Dat is
De gantsche H. Schrifture,
vervattende alle de Boecken
des Ouden ende de Nieuwen
TESTAMENTS:

Van nieuws uyt D. M. Luthers Hoogh-
Duytsche Bibel inde Neder-landsche
tale getrouwelijck over-geset, tot dienst
van de Christelijcke Gemeynten, d'ons
veranderde Augsburgsche Confessie
toegedaen in dese
Neder- landen.

In March of 2003, the story of the James Ossuary and the Jehoash Inscription took a surprising turn. The Israeli police raided Oded Golan's apartment and office. They discovered that Golan was owner of *both* the Jehoash Inscription and the James Ossuary. Furthermore, Israeli authorities strongly suspected Golan was more than just a collector of Bible antiquities. According to authorities, he was also a forger.

The Israel Antiquities Authority ordered a thorough investigation of the James Ossuary. They gathered a panel of experts on epigraphy and scientific dating. They agreed at a verdict: the ossuary itself was ancient, but the inscription carved into the side was modern. The proof was in the patina, the covering of dirt and foreign materials that forms on the surface of an ancient object. Archaeological finds do not emerge from centuries of burial all shiny and clean. Patina verifies that objects are actually ancient. On the James Ossuary, genuine patina covered most of the surface. However, someone had cut the inscription through the patina. A forger had done this recently.

Two years after it was found, very few biblical scholars still say the James Ossuary is genuine. The vast majority of archaeologists say both the James Ossuary and the Jehoash Inscription are forgeries. Neil Asher Silberman and Yuval Goren, writing in *Archaeology*, draw some sobering conclusions: "Sadly, the whole affair of the 'greatest' archaeological discoveries of the century had precisely the opposite effect its passionate promoters intended." They conclude it harmed public confidence that archaeology could prove the Bible to be true.

FAKES & FINDS

FORGING AN ANCIENT ARTIFACT: IT IS EASIER THAN YOU MIGHT THINK

Numerous antiquity stores sell alleged ancient biblical artifacts. Let the buyer beware! The Jehoash Inscription and James Ossuary prove that even the experts can be fooled by forgeries—at least for a time. Modern technology makes it much easier to reproduce ancient objects and ancient styles of writing. Today, the only way an object can be proved genuine is to record where and when the object was found. Archaeology must remain in the hands of archaeologists—tomb raiders and forgers destroy our knowledge of the past.

THE SILVER SCROLL

Fortunately, not all stories in biblical archaeology have such a sad ending. In September of 2004, scientists at the University of California applied the latest scientific dating methods to a tiny piece of rolled-up silver. Dr. Gabriel Barkay, archaeologist at Israel's Bar-Ilan University, had found the silver scroll in an ancient burial site. It contained the words of the *birkat kohanim*, the priestly blessing found in Numbers 6:24–26 of the Hebrew Bible. Barkay said the burial was from the seventh century BCE. That meant it was the oldest existing portion of any part of the Bible. Furthermore, it disproved claims by biblical minimalists that authors wrote the Bible later in Israel's history.

"The Lord bless you and keep you; The Lord make his face to shine upon you and be gracious to you: The Lord lift up his countenance upon you, and give you peace."

—the Priestly Blessing, Numbers 6:24–26

In the wake of the James Ossuary and Jehoash Inscription forgeries, archaeologists are cautious about discoveries claimed as evidence proving the Bible. Some experts said the silver scroll was actually from a much later period than Barkay claimed.

As experts at the University of California scrutinized the scroll, much was at stake. Was it as old as claimed? Would it verify that this part of the Bible dated to Israel's ancient history? The scientists finally announced the results of their research: the scroll dated to 600 BCE. It was indeed the oldest evidence of a Bible text.

At a time when the public is jaded and cynical, the silver scroll serves as a reminder of the best aspects of Bible archaeology. It was also an encouraging example of international teamwork. An Israeli archaeologist and U.S. scientists worked together to discover the truth concerning an ancient artifact.

The silver scroll also illustrates that archaeology can still have a positive impact on religious faith: 2,600 years ago, Jewish believers buried a loved one with the words of the birkat kohanim. Those words must have been important to his family and friends at this time of grief and loss. In the twenty-first century, Jewish faithful still hear these same words recited by a rabbi when loved ones are placed in the grave. The words of the silver scroll form a bridge between believers of ancient times and those of today. They are a reminder of the enduring power of faith.

Batey, Richard A. *Jesus & the Forgotten City: New Light on Sepphoris and the Urban World of Jesus.* Grand Rapids, Mich.: Baker Book House, 1992.

Feiler, Bruce. *Abraham: A Journey to the Heart of Three Faiths.* New York: HarperCollins, 2002.

Humphreys, Colin J. *The Miracles of Exodus: A Scientist's Discovery of the Extraordinary Natural Causes of the Biblical Exodus.* New York: HarperCollins, 2003.

Knopf, Alfred A., Eds. *The Holy Land.* New York: Knopf, 1995.

Metzger, Bruce, David Goldstein, and John Ferguson. *Great Events of Bible Times: A Fully Illustrated, Exciting Journey Back to the People and Places of the Bible.* New York: Barnes & Noble, 1998.

Page, Charles R., and Carl A. Volz. *The Land and the Book: An Introduction to the World of the Bible.* Nashville, Tenn.: Abingdon, 1993.

Pelligrino, Charles. *Return to Sodom and Gomorrah: From the Location of the Garden of Eden to the Parting of the Red Sea—Solving the Bible's Ancient Mysteries Through Archaeological Discovery.* New York: Avon Books, 1994.

Ryan, William, and Walter Pitman. *Noah's Flood: The New Scientific Discoveries About the Event that Changed History.* New York: Touchstone, 1998.

Wilson, Ian. *Before the Flood: The Biblical Flood as a Real Event and How It Changed the Course of Civilization.* New York: St. Martins, 2002.

FOR MORE INFORMATION

Bible archaeology articles from
Bible and Interpretation
www.bibleinterp.com/articles.htm

Bible History Online
www.bible-history.com/
links.php?cat=5&sub=57&cat_na
me=Ancient+Near+East&subcat
_name=Archaeology+%26+Sites

Bible Places.com
www.bibleplaces.com/index.htm

The Bible and History on
Campus Program.com
www.campusprogram.com/
reference/en/wikipedia/t/th/
the_bible_and_history.html

Har Karkom: 20 Years of Biblical
Archaeology by Emmanuel Anati
www.harkarkom.com/

The Jewish Magazine
Ancient Jewish History Archives
www.jewishmag.com/jimmenu/
ancient.htm

Think Tank—PBS
What Do We Know About the Bible?
www.pbs.org/thinktank/
transcript1019.html

Top Ten Archaeological Discoveries
of the Twentieth Century Relating
to the Biblical World
biblicalstudies.info/top10/schoville.htm

Publisher's note:
The Web sites listed on this page were active at the time of publication. The publisher is not responsible for Web sites that have changed their addresses or discontinued operation since the date of publication. The publisher will review and update the Web-site list upon each reprint.

Abraham 34–41
Albright, William F. 15, 84
ancient Israel 66–68
archaeologists vs. tomb raiders 12–13
Assyrians 73–74, 76

Babylon 77, 78
Ballard, Robert 31
Barkay, Dr. Gabriel 106–107
Battle of Jericho 54, 56, 57
biblical minimalists 16–17, 19, 106

Canaanites 63
Church of the Holy Sepulcher 97, 99
cuneiform 25, 40–41

dating systems 28
Dead Sea Scrolls 82, 84–85, 87–88, 90
Dome of the Rock 70, 73

Essenes 87

Feiler, Bruce 48
Fertile Crescent 38, 41
Freedman, Noel 16–17, 19

Gilgamesh Epic 25, 27
Glueck, Nelson 15

history of biblical archaeology 13,
    15–16
Holy of Holies 70

Institute for Creation Research (ICR)
    30
Iraq 77, 78, 81

The James Ossuary 100, 102–103, 105,
    106
Jehoash Inscription 103, 105, 106, 107
Jerusalem 66–68, 70, 73–74, 76, 97
Jesus (Yeshua) 90, 93–94, 97, 99
Joshua 54–63
    invasion of the Promised Land 57,
    60

Kenyon, Dame Kathleen 15–16, 21,
    56–57

Lawrence, Thomas 15

Marrero, Captain Emilio 77
Moses 42–53
Mount Sinai 51–52

Noah's ark 22–33
Noble Sanctuary 70

Petrie, Sir Flinders 13, 15

Queen of Sheba 64, 71
The Qumran community 87

Rawlinson, Henry 25

the silver scroll 106–107
Solomon 66–68, 70, 76

Tel Jericho 56

Western Wall 70
Woolley, Sir Leonard 15, 17, 27, 30, 41

PICTURE CREDITS

The illustrations in RELIGION AND MODERN CULTURE are photo montages made by Dianne Hodack. They are a combination of her original mixed-media paintings and collages, the photography of Benjamin Stewart, various historical public-domain artwork, and other royalty-free photography collections.

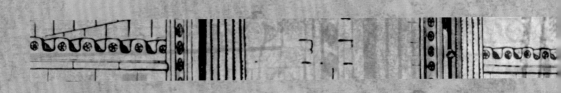

AUTHOR: Kenneth McIntosh is a freelance writer living in Flagstaff, Arizona. He has a master's degree in theology and has spoken on many occasions about the Bible and history. Formerly, he spent a decade teaching junior high school in Los Angeles, and he spent three weeks in 1997 on an archaeological study tour of Israel, Sinai, and Jordan. Kenneth enjoys visiting Native American archaeological sites in the deserts and mountains around his home.

CONSULTANT: Dr. Marcus J. Borg is the Hundere Distinguished Professor of Religion and Culture in the Philosophy Department at Oregon State University. Dr. Borg is past president of the Anglican Association of Biblical Scholars. Internationally known as a biblical and Jesus scholar, the *New York Times* called him "a leading figure among this generation of Jesus scholars." He is the author of twelve books, which have been translated into eight languages. Among them are *The Heart of Christianity: Rediscovering a Life of Faith* (2003) and *Meeting Jesus Again for the First Time* (1994), the best-selling book by a contemporary Jesus scholar.

CONSULTANT: Dr. Robert K. Johnston is Professor of Theology and Culture at Fuller Theological Seminary in Pasadena, California, having served previously as Provost of North Park University and as a faculty member of Western Kentucky University. The author or editor of thirteen books and twenty-five book chapters (including *The Christian at Play*, 1983; *The Variety of American Evangelicalism*, 1991; *Reel Spirituality: Theology and Film in Dialogue*, 2000; *Life Is Not Work/Work Is Not Life: Simple Reminders for Finding Balance in a 24/7 World*, 2000; *Finding God in the Movies: 33 Films of Reel Faith*, 2004; and *Useless Beauty: Ecclesiastes Through the Lens of Contemporary Film*, 2004), Johnston is the immediate past president of the American Theological Society, an ordained Protestant minister, and an avid bodysurfer.